I0820078

SCARY AMERICA

pil
Publications International, Ltd.

Written by J.K. Kelley and James Willis

Images from CardCow.com, Dreamstime, FloridaMemory.com, The Library of Congress, The New York Public Library, Shutterstock.com, and Wikipedia

Louis Weber, CEO
Publications International, Ltd.
8140 Lehigh Avenue
Morton Grove, IL 60053

ISBN: 978-1-63938-981-0

Manufactured in China.

8 7 6 5 4 3 2 1

Contents

Introduction

Not all hauntings are sinister and not all are as friendly as the caricatured Casper, but most—no matter the situation—are able to bring on a severe case of the howling fantods. There's something wrong here, but what? You may know there's an eldritch presence in your house, but what are you going to do? Move out? Address the enigma to try to agree on a peaceful living arrangement? Try to turn a blind eye and ignore all of the signs? Unfortunately, it's never that easy. You might need to call the paranormal experts and historians to get the real answer you're looking for.

Most places across the nation have a complex history that is swept under the rug by the broom of time, but not everything wants to or can be forgotten. People are attached to their surroundings and their family. They identify with their home, their neighborhood, their region, and their loved ones. They attach themselves to this world and they can't let go once they give up the ghost. They're left in the liminal space of being an ethereal being in a material world. Is there an afterlife? Is there a heaven and hell? Are the spirits of the deceased still present on this plane because they still need to accomplish something before they can move on? Who knows? But more and more people are beginning to believe that these entities are real.

Whether they are the vestiges of our ancestors spectrally guarding us, or something more sinister looking to take advantage of our physical being, they undoubtedly inhabit the spaces around us. From the East Coast to the West and the Midwest to the Deep South, the history of America still lives. Historic battlefields are still marched on by regiments from the other side. Beautiful mansions still house the ancestral heads of the estate. Suburbs and small communities tremble under the pressure of their troubled pasts. There is no escaping history, especially when it's still present everywhere around us. *Haunted America* roams across the nation to highlight these paranormal hotspots that are scattered from coast to coast. Get to know the signs and inform yourself of the taboo, unspoken history that surrounds you.

Old Montana Prison

Inmates Serve Life Sentences (Deer Lodge, Montana)

In 2010, a *Ghost Lab* episode titled "No Escape" depicted Brad and Barry Klinge's (founders of Everyday Paranormal) visit to the prison. A wealth of high-tech ghost-hunting equipment helped the investigators uncover supernatural phenomena ranging from mysterious whispers and the sound of footsteps in empty rooms and hallways to objects flying through the air.

In 1871, the Old Montana Prison opened its gates in Deer Lodge after citizens of the territory realized that laws needed to be enforced and the wilder elements of the region needed to be punished. Like many other prisons of the day, this facility soon became overcrowded, which led to sickness, poor living conditions, prisoner unrest, and the taut emotions that lead to restless spirits and residual hauntings.

No Escape

The year 1890 marked the beginning of the Conley era—a time when prison warden Frank Conley ruled with an iron fist and put his prisoners to work. But Conley also made significant improvements to both the prison itself and the lives of the inmates. He even established camps that sent the prisoners outside to work in the community.

However, this outside work was a privilege, and in 1908, two prisoners who were not allowed this freedom decided to take matters into their own hands. Their attempted escape resulted in the murder of the deputy prison warden and 103 stitches in the back and neck of Warden Conley. The two would-be escapees were hanged in the prison yard for their crime.

While touring the old prison, one can almost imagine the place as it was in the old days. Many people report hearing the shuffling of cards in the cellblocks, as well as mumbled voices and footsteps. Arguments have even been known to break out between people who aren't visible.

After that, the prison underwent many changes, including the end of prisoners working outside the facility, the addition of a women's prison, and the creation of a license plate manufacturing plant.

In 1959, the Old Montana Prison experienced a riot that lasted for three days and nights. Several inmates attempted to escape by holding the warden hostage and killing the deputy warden on the spot. After the National Guard was called in to end the melee, the two ringleaders died in a murder/suicide.

Several ghosts are known to haunt the prison grounds, and many visitors—especially psychics and ghost hunters who are sensitive to the spirit world—have experienced odd and sinister sensations. Some have even reported feeling physically ill.

Living With the Ghosts

Museum Director Julia Brewer is rather matter-of-fact about the hauntings in the old prison. After all, she has smelled burning flesh in her office for the better part of a decade, so you could say that she's a believer.

Brewer leads many of the groups that tour the facility, so she knows most of the prison lore. She also knows how to treat the spirits, and cautions visitors to treat the dead with respect...or else face the consequences.

A place known as the Death Tower produces a high level of otherworldly energy—it's where inmates Jerry Myles and Lee Smart died in a murder/suicide during the 1959 riot. A place called the Steam Hole carries some heavy energy of its own. Prisoners who were deemed unruly were often sent there; at least one prisoner died in the Steam Hole under suspicious circumstances, and another inmate took his own life there by hanging himself from a pipe.

Shadows and ghostly figures are common sights at the museum, and some visitors have reported seeing objects flying through the air in violent, threatening ways. People have also experienced a myriad of emotions and sensations: Some have reported feeling deep sadness or dread overtake them. And even more frightening, other visitors to the prison have perceived that someone or something is choking or attacking them.

Playful Spirits

A couple of ghosts are even known to hang around the museum's gift shop. One is the spirit of an inmate named Calvin, who was beaten to death in a corner of the room when it was an industrial area of the prison. Now the site houses a shelf of dolls, perhaps to neutralize the violence. A spirit that the staff refers to as "Stinker" also frequents the gift shop. The jokester of the pair, he likes to play pranks, such as moving merchandise around.

You'd think that ghosts would stick to their old haunts within the prison, but another place on the grounds that definitely seems haunted is the Montana Auto Museum, which is located just outside the gift shop. Staffers and visitors have seen ghostly figures there, and people have heard car doors slam when no one else is around.

And then there's the spirit of a young girl that has been observed by visitors at the auto museum. When a group reached the building on one ghost tour, the leader invited any spirits to show themselves by turning on a flashlight; the playful ghost did. The group also asked her to move a chain that was cordoning off the cars; she did that too.

Tombstone Shadows

(Tombstone, Arizona)

In its heyday, Tombstone, Arizona, was known as "The Town Too Tough to Die." Apparently, its ghosts liked that moniker because there are so many spirits roaming its streets that Tombstone is a strong contender for the title of "Most Haunted Town in America." Here are a few of the most notable phantoms that still call this Wild West town home.

The Bird Cage Theatre

Anyplace where twenty-six people were violently killed is almost certain to be a spectral smorgasbord. Such is the case with Tombstone's infamously bawdy Bird Cage Theatre.

One of the most frequently seen apparitions at the Bird Cage is that of a man who carries a clipboard and wears striped pants and a card-dealer's visor. He's been known to suddenly appear on stage, glide across it, and then walk through a wall. Visitors have raved to the management about how authentic-looking the Wild West costumes look, only to be told that nobody at the Bird Cage dresses in period clothing.

One night, an employee watched on a security monitor as a vaporous woman in white walked slowly through the cellar long after closing time. And although smoking and drinking are now prohibited at the Bird Cage, the scents of cigar smoke and whiskey still linger there. Visitors also hear unexplained sounds, such as a woman singing, a female sighing, glasses clinking, and cards shuffling, as if the ghosts are trying to finish a game that's gone on for far too long.

The Crystal Palace Saloon was restored in 1964 to its 1881 condition, including the forty-five-foot mahogany bar, Victorian ceiling lamps, and patterned wood floor.

Virgil Earp

A man in a long black frock coat stands on a sidewalk in Tombstone; the people who see him assume that he's a re-enactor in this former rough-and-tumble Wild West town. But as he starts across the street, a strange thing happens: He vanishes in mid-stride. Only then do people realize that they've just seen one of the many ghosts that haunt this legendary town.

It is usually assumed that the man in the black coat is the ghost of U.S. Deputy Marshal Virgil Earp, who may be reliving one of his life's darkest moments. On December 28, 1881, he was shot and wounded when outlaws who sought revenge for the infamous Gunfight at the O.K. Corral two months prior ambushed him. Virgil survived the attack, but his left arm was permanently maimed.

Morgan Earp

In March 1882, another group of outlaws—who were also seeking revenge for the Gunfight at the O.K. Corral—gunned down Morgan Earp, the brother of noted lawmen Virgil and Wyatt Earp. Morgan was shot in the back and killed while playing pool. Some say that you can still hear his dying words whispered at the location where he was murdered.

The tombstone of the outlaws killed at the Gunfight at the O.K. Corral by lawmen Virgil, Morgan, and Wyatt Earp along with Doc Holliday. The gunfight was the culmination of a feud between the outlaws and the lawmen over the lawmen's crackdown on illegal activities in 1881.

Big Nose Kate

Big Nose Kate was the girlfriend of gunslinger Doc Holliday, a friend of the Earps. Her ghost is reportedly responsible for the footsteps and snatches of whispered conversation that swirl through the Crystal Palace Saloon. Lights there turn on and off by themselves, and gambling wheels sometimes spin for no reason, causing speculation that, just as in life, Kate prefers the company of rowdy men.

It would almost defy belief if Tombstone's legendary Boothill Graveyard wasn't haunted, but not to worry: The final resting place of so many who were violently taken from this life is said to harbor many restless spirits, including that of Billy Clanton, one of the victims of the Gunfight at the O.K. Corral. Clanton's apparition has been seen rising from his grave and walking toward town. Strange lights and sounds are also said to come from the cemetery.

Swamper

Big Nose Kate's Saloon was originally the Grand Hotel, and a man known as Swamper used to work there as a handyman. He lived in the basement, not far from some of the town's silver mines, so when he wasn't working, Swamper dug a tunnel to one of the mines and began supplementing his income with silver nuggets. After all the effort that he'd put into obtaining the silver, Swamper was not about to let it go easily...not even after he died. He reportedly haunts Big Nose Kate's Saloon; perhaps he's still hanging around to protect his loot, which has never been found. Naturally, he's often spotted in the basement, but he also likes to show up in photos taken by visitors.

Yuma Territorial Prison
Holds Inmates for Life (Yuma, Arizona)

What could be worse than being locked in a prison cell for life? How about being locked in a prison that you were forced to help build? That's what happened to the first seven inmates at the Yuma Territorial Prison back in 1876. Is it any wonder that the place is considered one of the most haunted locations in Arizona?

There were no minimum- or maximum-security prisons in the 1800s, so inmates at the Yuma Prison ranged from petty thieves to murderers. By the time the prison closed in 1909, more than 3,000 convicts had been held within its walls. Compared to today's standards, prison life back then was hard. Each cell measured only nine feet by nine feet, and it was not uncommon for the indoor temperature to reach 110 degrees in the summer. A punishment known as the "Dark Cell" was similar to what we now call solitary confinement. And a ball and chain were used to punish prisoners who tried to escape. It must have worked because plenty of souls never left this place.

Although the Yuma Territorial Prison only operated for thirty-three years, it is home to its fair share of paranormal activity. This begs the questions: Was the prison built so soundly that for many, there was no escape, even in death? Or did the inmates just give up and choose to stay there forever?

The Good, the Bad, and the Ghostly

Despite the brutal conditions, a library and educational programs were available to inmates, and a prison clinic even gave them access to medical care. But the jail soon became overcrowded, and in such close quarters, tuberculosis ran rampant. During its thirty-three-year history, 111 prisoners died there, many from TB; eight were gunned down in unsuccessful escape attempts.

From 1910 to 1914, the former prison building housed Yuma High School. Considering the restless souls that were left over from the structure's days as a prison, it probably did not make for the best educational experience. During the Great Depression, homeless families sought shelter within its walls. And later, local residents who wanted to have a little piece of Arizona history "borrowed" stones from the building's walls for their personal construction projects.

In June 2005, Arizona Desert Ghost Hunters spent the night at the Yuma Territorial Prison and were convinced the place was indeed haunted given the evidence they gathered. Photos taken of the guard tower and in Cell 14 both show suspicious activity: An orb can be seen near the tower and a misty figure is clearly visible in Cell 14, where inmate John Ryan hung himself in 1903. The investigators also captured EVPs (electronic voice phenomena) in Cell 14, where a voice said, "Get away," and in the Dark Cell, where a male spirit told the group to "Get out of here."

In its Wild West heyday, the Yuma Territorial Prison held many notable inmates like Burt Alvord, William J. Flake, Pearl Hart, Frank Leslie, Ricardo Flores Magón, and Pete Spence.

Solitary Spirits

Today, all that remains of the former Yuma Territorial Prison are some cells, the main gate, a guard tower, the prison cemetery—and the ghosts. A museum is located on the site, and visitors and employees report that spirits have settled there as well. Lights turn on and off randomly; objects are moved from one place to another; and once, the coins from the gift shop's cash register leaped into the air and then fell back into place.

The Dark Cell is also a focal point for ghostly activity: The restless spirits of prisoners who were sent there for disobeying rules are thought to linger. At least two inmates were transferred directly from that cell to an insane asylum, but whether anyone actually died there is unknown. It makes for a few unsettled spirits, though, doesn't it?

Linda Offeney, an employee at the prison site, once reported feeling an unseen presence in the Dark Cell. And a tourist who visited the prison in the 1930s had her photo taken near the Dark Cell; the picture looked perfectly normal—except for the ghostly figure of a man standing behind her within the cell.

Offeney also tells the story of a writer for *Arizona Highways* magazine who witnessed the hauntings: The journalist wanted to spend two days and two nights in the cell just as prisoners would have—in the dark, with only bread and water. She only made it a few hours before she called for assistance, explaining that she couldn't shake the feeling that something was in the cell with her.

Finished in 1909, the Stanley Hotel provided guests with hydraulic elevators, telephones in every room, electric and gas lighting, running water, and a shuttle service to transport the guests from the hotel's remote grounds to the train station twenty miles away.

Spirits Shine on at the Stanley Hotel (Estes Park, Colorado)

The Stanley Hotel—a beautiful Georgian-style resort in Estes Park, Colorado—was the inspiration for the Overlook Hotel in Stephen King's famous novel *The Shining* and the movie adaptation, which starred Jack Nicholson. Fortunately, unlike at King's fictional inn, the ghosts of the Stanley Hotel are not malicious. But rest assured, there are definitely ghosts at this famous hotel.

How It All Began

In 1903, F. O. Stanley—inventor of the Stanley Steamer automobile—was suffering from tuberculosis and was told that he had just months to live. That year, Stanley and his wife, Flora, visited Estes Park hoping to find some relief in the thin mountain air. They fell in love with its majestic Rocky Mountain landscape and decided to move there permanently. Shortly thereafter, construction began on the Stanley Hotel, which was completed in 1909. (Stanley died in 1940 at the ripe old age of ninety-one, so apparently the mountain air did the trick.)

Nestled in the mountains, the resort offers a spectacular view. Many notable guests have stayed at the Stanley Hotel, including John Philip Sousa, President Theodore Roosevelt, Japanese royalty, members of the Hollywood set—including Jim Carrey, Rebecca De Mornay, and Elliott Gould—and, of course, writer Stephen King.

Friendly Ghosts

King stayed in Room 237, which is the haunted room in *The Shining*. However, most of the paranormal activity at the Stanley seems to occur on the fourth floor, specifically in Room 418. There, guests have heard children laughing and playing, but when they complain that the children are too loud, no children are ever found.

In Room 407, a ghost likes to play with the lights. However, it's apparently a reasonable spook: When guests ask it to turn the lights back on, it does.

Freelan Oscar Stanley, inventor of the Stanley Steamer and the hotel's founder, can reportedly be seen wandering around the hotel with his wife long after they died in the mid-20th century.

During his stay, Stephen King alerted the staff that a young boy on the second floor was calling for his nanny. Of course, the staff members at the Stanley were well aware of the ghostly boy, who had been spotted throughout the hotel many times over the years.

But the two most prominent spirits at the resort are those of F. O. Stanley and his wife. Flora makes her presence known by playing the piano in the ballroom. Even those who haven't seen her claim to hear piano music coming from the ballroom when it's empty, and some have seen the piano keys move up and down of their own accord.

F. O. Stanley's specter most often manifests in the lobby, the bar, and the billiard room, which were apparently his favorite spots in the building when he was alive.

A Ghostly Visitor

When Jason Hawes and Grant Wilson from the television show *Ghost Hunters* stayed at the Stanley Hotel in 2006, their investigation hit paranormal pay dirt. Hawes stayed in Room 401—purportedly one of the most haunted guest rooms—and set up a video camera to record anything that occurred while he was asleep. Although the picture is dark, the camera captured the distinct sounds of a door opening and glass breaking—all while Hawes was sound asleep. When he got up to investigate, he noticed that the closet door had been opened and a glass on the nightstand was broken. Later, the camera recorded the closet door closing—and latching—with no humans in sight.

Wilson had his own paranormal experience in Room 1302: He was sitting at a table with some other team members when the table lifted off the ground and crashed back down—all of its own accord. When the group tried to raise the table, they found it to be so heavy that it took several people to lift it even a few inches.

The Stanley Hotel offers ghost tours to educate visitors about the paranormal activity within its walls. Or if you'd rather just stay in your room, you could always watch a movie—*The Shining* runs continuously on the guest-room televisions.

Spirits Aboard the *Queen Mary* (Long Beach, California)

Once considered a grand jewel of the ocean, the decks of the *Queen Mary* played host to such rich and famous guests as Clark Gable, Charlie Chaplin, Laurel and Hardy, and Elizabeth Taylor. Today, the *Queen Mary* is permanently docked, but she still hosts some mysterious, ghostly passengers!

Following the surrender of Germany, the *Queen Mary* was used to carry American troops and GI war brides to the United States and Canada, before returning to England for conversion back to a luxury liner.

The *Queen Mary* Goes to War

The *Queen Mary* took her maiden voyage in May 1936, but a change came in 1940 when the British government pressed the ocean liner into military service. She was given a coat of gray paint and was turned into a troop transport vessel. The majestic dining salons became mess halls and the cocktail bars, cabins, and staterooms were filled with bunks. Even the swimming pools were boarded over and crowded with cots for the men. The ship was so useful to the Allies that Hitler offered a $250,000 reward and hero status to the U-Boat commander who could sink her. None of them did.

Although the *Queen Mary* avoided enemy torpedoes during the war, she was unable to avoid tragedy. On October 2, 1942, escorted by the cruiser HMS *Curacoa* and several destroyers, the *Queen Mary* was sailing on the choppy North Atlantic near Ireland. She was carrying about 15,000 American soldiers.

Danger from German vessels was always present, but things were quiet until suddenly, before anyone could act, the *Queen Mary*'s massive bow smashed into the *Curacoa*. There was no way to slow down, no time for warning, and no distress calls to the men onboard. They had only seconds to react before their ship was sliced in two. Within minutes, both sections of the ship plunged below the surface of the icy water, carrying the crew with them. Of the *Curacoa*'s 439-man crew, 338 of them perished on that fateful day. The *Queen Mary* suffered only minor damage and there were no injuries to her crew.

After that, the *Queen Mary* served unscathed for the remainder of the war.

Last Days of an Ocean Liner

After the war, the *Queen Mary* and her sister ship, the *Queen Elizabeth*, were the preferred method of transatlantic travel for the rich and famous. But by the 1960s, airplane travel was faster and cheaper, and so, in late 1967, the *Queen Mary* steamed away from England for the last time. Her decks and staterooms were filled with curiosity seekers and wealthy patrons who wanted to be part of the ship's final voyage. She ended her thirty-nine-day journey in Long Beach, California, where she was permanently docked as a floating hotel, convention center, museum, and restaurant. She is now listed on the National Register of Historic Places and is open to visitors year-round.

The HMS *Curacoa* in 1918, fourteen years before its accidental demise when it collided with the *Queen Mary* in the North Atlantic near Ireland.

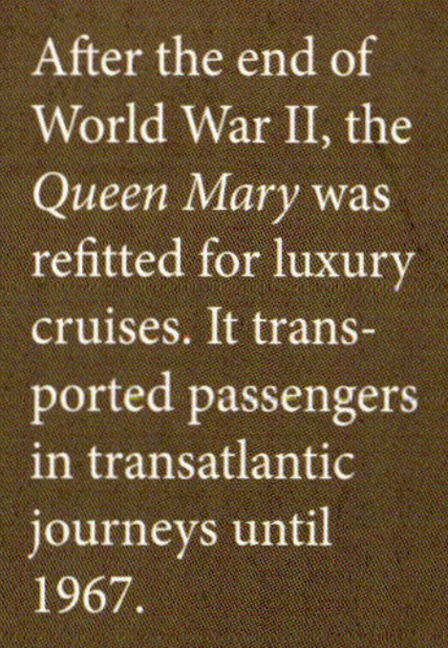

After the end of World War II, the *Queen Mary* was refitted for luxury cruises. It transported passengers in transatlantic journeys until 1967.

The Haunted *Queen Mary*

The *Queen Mary* has seen much tragedy and death, so it's no surprise that the ship plays host to a number of ghosts. Because of the sheer number of passengers who have walked her decks, accidents were bound to happen. One such mishap occurred on July 10, 1966, when John Pedder, an engine room worker, was crushed to death when an automatic door closed on him.

There have been other reported deaths onboard, as well. For instance, during the war, when the ship was used for troop transport, a brawl broke out in one of the galleys and a cook was allegedly shoved into a hot oven, where he burned to death. There are also reports of a woman drowning in the ship's swimming pool and stories of passengers falling overboard.

Another strange death onboard was that of Senior Second Officer William Stark, whose ghost has often been spotted on deck and in his former quarters. Stark died after drinking lime juice mixed with cleaning solution, which he mistook for gin. He realized his error, and while he joked about it, he called the ship's doctor. Unfortunately, though, Stark soon felt the effects of the poison. As the young officer's condition worsened, he lapsed into a coma and died on September 22, 1949.

Witnesses have also encountered a spectral man in gray overalls who has been seen below deck. He has dark hair and a long beard and is believed to be a mechanic or maintenance worker from the 1930s.

Another friendly spirit, dubbed "Miss Turner," is believed to have been a switchboard operator on the ship. A ghostly woman known as "Mrs. Kilburn" wears a gray uniform with starched white cuffs. She was once in charge of the stewardesses and bellboys, and she's still watching over the comings and goings on the ship. And although it is unknown who the ship's "Lady in White" might be, she haunts the exhibit hall known as the Queen's Salon and is normally seen wearing a white, backless evening gown. Witnesses say she dances alone near the grand piano as if listening to music only she can hear, then vanishes.

Security guards, staff members, and visitors have also reported doors unlocking, opening, and closing on their own, often triggering security alarms. Other unexplained occurrences include phantom voices and footsteps, banging and hammerings sounds, cold spots, inexplicable winds that blow through closed-off areas, and lights that turn on and off.

During a tour of the ship, one guest felt someone tugging on her purse and sweater and stroking her hair. Cold chills crept down her spine when she realized there was no one near her at the time!

In 1967, some twenty-five years after the tragic accident with the *Curacoa*, a marine engineer working inside the ship heard the terrible sound of two ships colliding. He even heard screams and shredding steel. Did the terrible events of 1942 somehow leave an impression on the atmosphere of this grand old ship? Or worse, is the crew of the *Curacoa* still doomed to relive that fateful October afternoon for eternity?

The *Queen Mary* is permanently moored in Long Beach, California, and serves as a hotel, museum, and event facility.

Ghost tours on the ship allow guests to access restricted areas of the ship where not even the history tours are allowed to enter.

In 2017, a report on the condition of the ship claimed that nearly $300 million would be needed to prevent further corrosion of the ship's hull and exhibition-area supports.

A Favorite Celebrity Haunt
(San Diego, California)

San Diego's grand Hotel del Coronado sparkles in the California sun. It's a popular seaside resort, a National Historic Landmark, and a very haunted hotel. Affectionately called "the Del," the hotel is proud of Kate Morgan, its resident ghost. Her story is just one of the hotel's many spine-tingling tales.

The Hotel Del Coronado, one of the last standing examples of wooden Victorian beach resorts in America, was the largest resort in the world when it was completed in 1888.

The Mysterious Mrs. Morgan

On November 24, 1892, Kate Morgan checked into the Hotel del Coronado under the name Lottie A. Bernard from Detroit. She looked pale and said she wasn't feeling well. She mentioned that she was planning to meet her brother, a doctor. After a few days, the staff began to worry.

The mysterious woman had checked in with no luggage. Her brother hadn't arrived, and she had barely left her room. On Monday, November 28, the woman went into town and purchased a gun. Her body was found early the next morning on stairs that led from the hotel to the beach. From the gunshot wound to her head, it appeared she had committed suicide. When police investigated, they found few personal belongings in her hotel room.

Guests enjoying the gardens, circa 1900.

Murder or Suicide?

After Kate's death, police determined that "Lottie A. Bernard" was an alias. They sent a sketch of her to newspapers, which described her as "the beautiful stranger." Further investigation uncovered that "Lottie" had been born Kate Farmer in Iowa, and married Tom Morgan in 1885.

Morgan was reputed to be a conman and a gambler. He allegedly worked the rails and enlisted Kate's help in stealing money from train passengers. According to a witness, somewhere between Los Angeles and San Diego, Kate and Morgan had an intense argument on a train. Morgan departed before reaching San Diego; Kate continued on the train and then checked into the Del.

Some people claim that the clues at the scene add up to murder rather than suicide. Attorney Alan May's 1990 book, *The Legend of Kate Morgan*, claims the bullet that killed Kate was a different caliber than the gun she'd purchased.

Haunting in Room 302

Whatever happened, Kate's ghost has lingered at the Del. She often manifests as eerie eyes and lips appearing in the mirror or reflected in the window of her room. Kate's spirit may be responsible for strange noises and unexplained breezes around her room as well. The curtains on closed windows billow for no reason, and lights and televisions turn themselves on and off. Kate also appears as a pale young woman in a black lace dress. A sweet fragrance lingers after her apparition disappears.

Kate stayed in Room 302. Later, during remodeling the hotel changed the room number to 3327. The haunted room is so popular that people ask for it as "the Kate Morgan room." The hotel welcomes questions about the ghost, and everyone treats Kate as an honored guest.

The Mysterious Maid

Room 3519 at the Del is also haunted, perhaps even more intensely than Kate's room.

In 1983, a Secret Service agent stayed in Room 3519 while guarding then-Vice President George H.W. Bush. The special agent bolted from the room in the middle of the night claiming that he'd heard unearthly gurgling noises and that the entire room seemed to glow.

The Secret Service agent may have encountered a ghost related to the Kate Morgan mystery. According to one legend, while Kate was at the hotel, a maid stayed in what would later be Room 3519. In some versions of the story, the maid was traveling with Kate; in others, the maid had simply befriended her. Whatever the connection between the two, the maid allegedly vanished the same morning Kate was found dead.

That's not the only ghost story connected with Room 3519. Another story goes that in 1888, the year the hotel was built, a wealthy man kept his mistress in that room. When the woman found out she was pregnant, she killed herself. Her body was removed from the Del, and nothing else is known about her, not even her name. Ghost hunters believe she is the one who causes the lights in the room to flicker and is responsible for the unexplained cold spot in front of the room's door.

The Hotel Del Coronado four years after the hotel's completion.

When the hotel was opened in 1888, it boasted nearly 400 guest rooms, but only 71 bathrooms (bathtubs) and 71 water closets (toilets). It might have been the premier resort on the West Coast at the time, but indoor plumbing was still a luxury that had not yet reached ubiquity.

The Blonde on the Beach

In recent years, some hotel guests have reported sightings of the ghost of Marilyn Monroe. She loved the Hotel del Coronado when she stayed there to film the movie *Some Like It Hot*. Monroe's ghost has appeared at several of her favorite places, including Hollywood's Roosevelt Hotel, where people see her in the lobby's mirror.

At the Del, Monroe is supposedly seen outdoors as a fleeting, translucent apparition near the door to the hotel or on the beach nearby. Those who see Monroe's ghost comment on her windswept blonde hair and her fringed shawl that flutters in the breeze. Others have allegedly heard her light giggle in the second and third floor hallways.

Whether they're from a rural farm or the silver screen, guests and ghosts love the Hotel del Coronado. If you choose to stay in one of its most haunted rooms, just remember that you're never alone.

The Curse of Griffith Park (Los Angeles, California)

The dark history of Griffith Park began in 1863, when it was called Rancho Los Feliz. That year, owner Don Antonio Feliz passed from this world, and many expected that his blind niece, Doña Petranilla, would inherit his fortune. Unbeknownst to Petranilla, however, local lawyer Don Antonio Coronel had visited Feliz to help him rewrite his will. When Feliz succumbed to smallpox, most of his wealth went to Coronel. Petranilla was outraged, and from the family adobe, she laid a curse upon the land that is still felt to this day.

A Curse Fit for a Colonel

Following Petranilla's curse, the Coronels and other subsequent owners were all plagued with misfortune and disease until Colonel Griffith J. Griffith, a wealthy industrialist, purchased the property. When Griffith acquired the land in 1882, opening a park was the last thing on his mind: His first order of business was to build housing developments on the land, but that venture soon failed. Griffith also allowed a small ostrich farm to open on the property, and surprisingly, it was quite successful. However, in 1884, storms plagued the area and the ostriches stampeded every night. Ranch hands claimed that the cause of the ruckus was a phantom rider that appeared in the rain. Some said that it was the ghost of Don Feliz, but others believed that it was Doña Petranilla, back from the dead to fulfill the curse that she imposed on the land. Regardless of who it was, Griffith refused to visit the property except at midday, and in 1896, to rid himself of the ghost once and for all, he donated 3,015 acres of his land to the city of Los Angeles.

However, that didn't stop the spirit from making appearances from time to time. In 1898, when the city's wealthy and influential residents gathered for a fiesta at Griffith Park, an ethereal horseback rider chased them out. Over the years, many visitors to the park have reported seeing this spirit sitting atop a horse and roaming the park's trails, or riding through the park at night.

Unfortunately, Griffith's mind deteriorated after that, and in 1903, he tried to kill his wife because he thought that she was conspiring against him with the Pope; he spent nearly two years in San Quentin for the crime. When he died in 1919, Colonel Griffith bequeathed his remaining fortune to the city of Los Angeles. If he relieved himself of the cursed property in an attempt to appease its restless spirits, the maneuver seems to have failed.

To Live and Die in Hollywood

In the 1930s, Griffith Park claimed another victim. Like so many others, Peg Entwistle had come to Hollywood to realize her dream of seeing her visage on the silver screen. However, after receiving poor reviews for her performance in her first motion picture, Entwistle concluded that her career was a failure. And so, on the night of September 16, 1932, she climbed to the top of the Hollywood sign's *H* and leaped to her death in the ravine below. A suicide note was found in her purse, and within days, she had achieved the fame that had eluded her in life.

Over the years, several hikers and park rangers have reported seeing a woman dressed in 1930s-era attire near the sign. And from time to time, a spectral blonde woman has been known to set off motion sensors located near the sign. When the rangers investigate, they notice the scent of gardenias.

Along with the 3,015 acres of land Griffith J. Griffith donated to the city of Los Angeles were funds to build an observatory on the land. The construction began in 1933, and the observatory opened to the public two years later.

The park is a massive mountainside complex that contains the universally recognized Hollywood sign, the Griffith Observatory, the former Grffith Park Zoo and now Los Angeles Zoo, the Greek Theater, and the Los Angeles Live Steamers Railroad Museum. The park is even home to one known mountain lion that has been photographed by motion-activated cameras.

The City of Angels' Lady in White

Park rangers spend more time in Griffith Park than anyone else, and they know that they're not alone. In their headquarters in the old Feliz adobe, the rangers have reportedly caught glimpses of a ghostly Hispanic woman who is dressed all in white. Most people seem to think that this is the tormented spirit of Doña Petranilla, the woman who originally cursed the land back in 1863. She died soon after placing the curse, and she is one of the property's oldest lost souls. In 1884, the worst of the storms that ripped through the area stripped most of the vegetation from the land. Around that time, Griffith's ranch hands witnessed the Lady in White cursing the land and all who lived on it, just as she had done in life. Some have reported hearing her wailing near the Los Angeles Zoo and the golf course, but her favorite haunt seems to be her former home. Although the park is closed overnight, Petranilla seems to prefer to make nocturnal appearances, and like her uncle and Colonel Griffith, she is sometimes seen on horseback going for a midnight ride.

Spending Eternity on "The Rock" (San Francisco, California)

From 1934 to 1963, during its reign as a federal prison, Alcatraz was not a facility for rehabilitating hardened criminals; it was a place of harsh punishment and limited privilege. Those who endured their stay were fortunate to leave with their sanity or—as many believe—their souls.

The Island of Pelicans

When the Spanish first explored the area in 1775, they dubbed the island La Isla de los Alcatraces, or "the Island of the Pelicans." What they found was a rocky piece of land that was completely uninhabited, sparsely vegetated, and surrounded by churning water and swift currents.

The U.S. military took over Alcatraz Island in 1850. For several decades, it was the army's first long-term prison, and it quickly gained a reputation for being a tough facility. The military used the island until 1934, when high operating costs coupled with the financial constraints of the Great Depression forced their exit.

America's Devil's Island

The rise of criminal activity in the 1920s and early 1930s put a new focus on Alcatraz. Federal authorities decided to construct an imposing, escape-proof prison that would strike fear into even the hardest criminals, and Alcatraz was the chosen site. In 1934, the Federal Bureau of Prisons took control of the facility and implemented a strict set of rules and regulations. The top guards and officers of the federal penal system were transferred to the island, and soon Alcatraz was transformed into an impregnable fortress.

Across the country, prison wardens were asked to send their worst inmates to Alcatraz. This included inmates with behavioral issues, those who had previously attempted to escape, and the most notorious criminals of the day, including Al Capone, George "Machine Gun" Kelly, Doc Barker (of the Ma Barker Gang), and Alvin "Creepy" Karpis. Life on The Rock was anything but luxurious. Each day was exactly the same, from chow times to work assignments. The routine never varied and was completely methodical. Compliance

Alcatraz Island not only houses the abandoned prison but also the oldest operating lighthouse on the West Coast of the U.S.

was expected, and the tough guards sometimes meted out severe punishment if rules were not followed.

If prisoners broke the rules, they could be sent to a punishment cell known as "The Hole." There were several of these cells, which were dreaded by the convicts. Here, men were stripped of all but their basic right to food. During the daytime, mattresses were taken away and steel doors blocked out any natural light. Prisoners might spend as long as nineteen days in The Hole in complete isolation. Time spent there usually meant psychological and physical abuse from the guards as well. Screams from hardened criminals could be heard echoing throughout the entire building in a stark warning to the other prisoners.

After time spent in The Hole, men often came out with pneumonia or arthritis after spending days or weeks on the cold cement floor with no clothing. Others came out devoid of their sanity. Some men never came out of The Hole alive.

Alcatraz and "Scarface" Al Capone

Al Capone arrived at Alcatraz in August 1934. He was fairly well behaved, but life on The Rock was not easy for the ex-crime boss. He was involved in a number of fights during his incarceration, was once stabbed with a pair of scissors, and spent some time in isolation while at Alcatraz.

Attempts on his life, beatings, and the prison routine itself took their toll on Capone. Seeking a diversion, he played the banjo in a prison band. Some legends say that Scarface spent most of his time strumming his banjo alone, hoping to avoid other prisoners. In reality, after more than three years in Alcatraz, Capone was on the edge of total insanity. He spent the last year of his federal sentence in the hospital ward, undergoing treatment for an advanced case of syphilis.

When Capone left Alcatraz, he definitely seemed worse for the wear. It appeared that The Rock (and his nasty case of syphilis) had completely broken him. In January 1939, he was transferred to another prison to serve out a separate sentence. Capone was released to his family and doctors in November 1939 and became a recluse at his Florida estate. He died, broken and insane, in 1947.

Al Capone was not the only inmate to lose his grip on reality at Alcatraz. While working in the prison garage, convicted bank robber Rufe Persful picked up an ax and chopped the fingers off his left hand. Laughing maniacally, he asked another prisoner to cut off his right hand as well. An inmate named Joe Bowers sustained a superficial wound when he tried to slash his own throat with a pair of broken eyeglasses. Ed Wutke, who was at Alcatraz for murder, managed to use a pencil sharpener blade to fatally cut through his jugular vein. These were not the only suicide attempts, and many other men suffered mental breakdowns at Alcatraz.

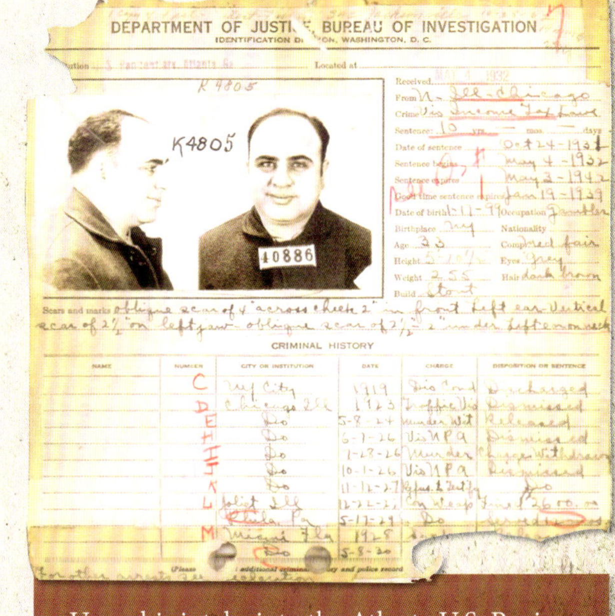

DEPARTMENT OF JUSTI[illegible], BUREAU OF INVESTIGATION
IDENTIFICATION DI[illegible]ON, WASHINGTON, D. C.

Located at

K4805

40886

Received MAY 4 1932
From N. Ill. Chicago
Crime Vio Income Tax Laws
Sentence: 10 yrs. — mos. — days
Date of sentence Oct 24-1931
Sentence begins May 4-1932
Sentence expires May 3-1942
Good time sentence expires Jan 19-1939
Date of birth 1-17-99 Occupation Gambler
Birthplace N.Y. Nationality
Age 33 Complexion fair
Height 5-10½ Eyes Grey
Weight 255 Hair dark brown
Build Stout

Scars and marks oblique scar of 4" across cheek 2" in front left ear. Vertical scar of 2½" on left jaw. oblique scar of 2½" 2" under left ear on neck

CRIMINAL HISTORY

NAME	NUMBER	CITY OR INSTITUTION	DATE	CHARGE	DISPOSITION OR SENTENCE
	C	N.Y. City	1919	Dis. Cond.	Discharged
	D	Chicago Ill	1923	Traffic Vio	Dismissed
	E	Do	5-8-24	Murder Wit	Released
	H	Do	6-7-26	Vio NPA	Dismissed
	I	Do	7-28-26	Murder	Charge Withdrawn
	J	Do	10-1-26	Vio NPA	Dismissed
	K	Do	11-12-27	[illegible]	Do
	L	Joliet Ill	12-22-2[illegible]	Con Weap	Fine $2600.00
		Phila. Pa	5-17-29	Do	[illegible]
	M	Miami Fla	1928	[illegible]	[illegible]
		Do	5-8-30		

Upon his intake into the Atlanta U.S. Penitentiary, 250-pound Capone was diagnosed with both syphilis and gonorrhoea. He also suffered from withdrawals and a perforated septum from his cocaine addiction. Capone was moved to Alcatraz because there were suspicions he was receiving special treatment from the guards in Atlanta. Neurosyphilis eventually led to Capone's mental deterioration which confined him to the penitentiary's hospital for the last year of his prison sentence.

Escapes From Alcatraz

During Alcatraz's twenty-nine years as a federal prison, thirty-four different men tried to escape the island in fourteen separate attempts. In almost every case, the escapees were killed or recaptured. Two escape attempts are particularly infamous.

In May 1946, six inmates captured a gun cage, obtained prison keys, and took over a cell house in less than an hour. Unfortunately for them, the only key they did not get was the one that would let them out of the cell building, which effectively grounded the escape plot. The prison break turned into a heated gunfight that led to the deaths of three of the escapees, as well as several guards. When it was over, two of the surviving escapees were sentenced to death and the third received a life sentence.

Though the 1946 incident may have been the most violent escape attempt at Alcatraz, it is not the most famous. That distinction belongs to a 1962 attempt by Frank Morris and brothers Clarence and John Anglin. Over several months, the men chipped away at the vent shafts in their cells using tools they had stolen from work sites. They also created makeshift rafts and inflatable life vests using raincoats. They even collected hair from the barbershop and made lifelike dummies to fool the guards on duty during the escape. Then, on the night of June 11, 1962, after making their way out of the prison, the trio boarded their rafts and set out into the cold waters of the bay, never to be seen again.

More than four decades later, it is still unclear whether or not the escapees survived. According to the Bureau of Prisons, the men are either missing or presumed drowned. The story of the escape was brought to the silver screen in the 1979 film *Escape from Alcatraz*, starring Clint Eastwood.

The A-Block of cells, also called "Michigan Avenue," was never used to hold inmates permanently but was used for temporary holding before inmates were transferred to other cellblocks. A-Block's military-prison design was never modernized and retains its spiral staircases, flat-strap iron bars, and key locks.

The Warden's House on Alcatraz Island is now in ruins after it was set on fire by Native Americans in the Occupation of Alcatraz on June 1, 1970.

The Haunted Prison

On March 23, 1963, less than a year after this last escape attempt, Alcatraz ended its run as a federal prison, and the island remained largely abandoned until the early 1970s. Congress placed the island under the purview of the National Park Service in 1972, and Alcatraz opened to the public in 1973. It is now one of the most popular historic sites in America.

In the daytime, the former prison bustles with the activity of tour guides and visitors, but at night, the buildings play host to some unexplainable phenomena. Many believe that some of those who served time on The Rock linger for eternity.

Accounts of hauntings have been widely reported since Alcatraz first shut its doors. Park service employees and visitors to Alcatraz report weird, ghostly encounters in the crumbling, old buildings. Unexplained clanging sounds, footsteps, and disembodied voices and screams are commonly heard coming from the empty corridors and long-abandoned cells. Some guides have reportedly witnessed strange events in certain areas of the prison, such as the infamous "holes," where prisoners suffered greatly.

But perhaps the most eerie sound is the faint banjo music sometimes heard in the shower room. Legend has it that Al Capone would often sit and strum his banjo in that spot rather than risk going out into the yard. Is it the broken spirit of Al Capone that creates this mournful melody on his phantom instrument? Or is it another ghostly inmate, unable to escape, even after death?

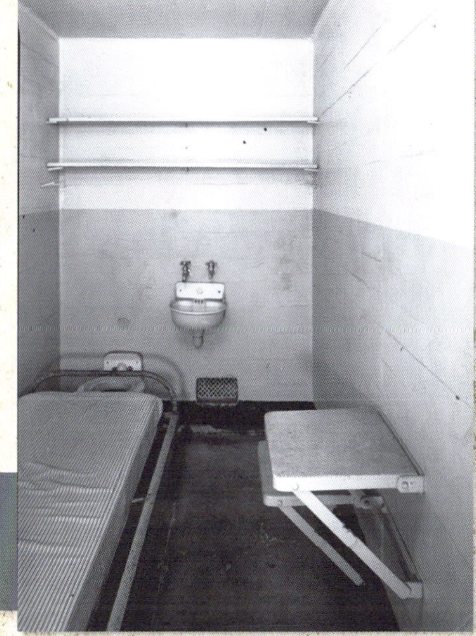

Each cell measured five feet by nine feet and featured a fold-up bunk, desk, chair, toilet, and sink.

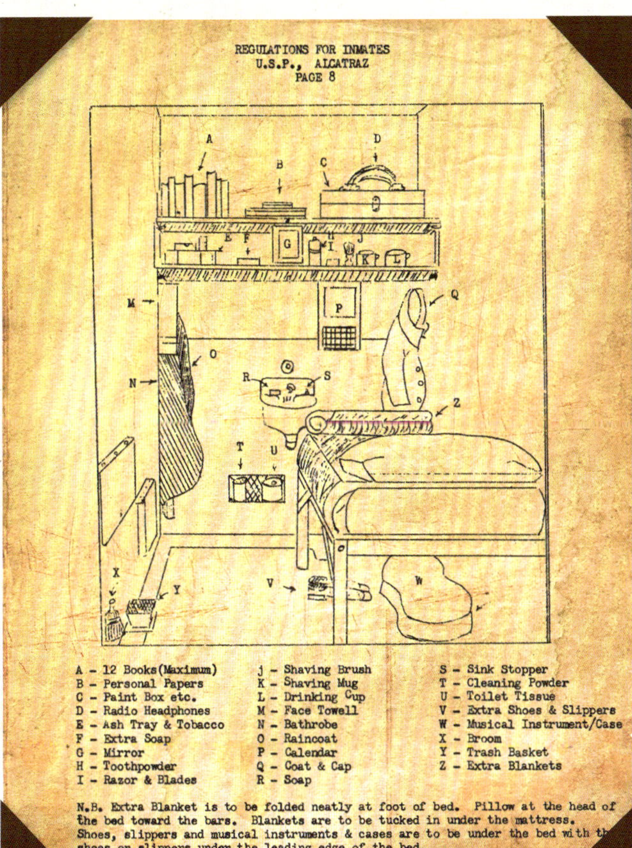

REGULATIONS FOR INMATES
U.S.P., ALCATRAZ
PAGE 8

A - 12 Books(Maximum)
B - Personal Papers
C - Paint Box etc.
D - Radio Headphones
E - Ash Tray & Tobacco
F - Extra Soap
G - Mirror
H - Toothpowder
I - Razor & Blades

j - Shaving Brush
K - Shaving Mug
L - Drinking Cup
M - Face Towell
N - Bathrobe
O - Raincoat
P - Calendar
Q - Coat & Cap
R - Soap

S - Sink Stopper
T - Cleaning Powder
U - Toilet Tissue
V - Extra Shoes & Slippers
W - Musical Instrument/Case
X - Broom
Y - Trash Basket
Z - Extra Blankets

N.B. Extra Blanket is to be folded neatly at foot of bed. Pillow at the head of the bed toward the bars. Blankets are to be tucked in under the mattress. Shoes, slippers and musical instruments & cases are to be under the bed with th shoes or slippers under the leading edge of the bed.

A page from the 1956 document "Institution Rules and Regulations of the United States Penitentiary, Alcatraz Island" that lays out the order in which inmates should have kept their cells.

Winchester Mystery House

(San Jose, California)

By the time she was twenty-two, Sarah Pardee was seriously popular—she spoke four languages, played the piano, and was exceedingly pretty. Nicknamed the "Belle of New Haven," she had her pick of suitors.

She chose a young man named William W. Winchester, the only son of Oliver Winchester, a stockholder with the successful New Haven Arms Company. When Sarah and William married in 1862, William had plans to expand the business by buying out some of his competition and introducing the repeating rifle, so named because its lever action allowed a gunman to fire many shots in succession. The gun became known as "The Gun That Won the West," and the now fabulously wealthy Winchester name was woven into the fabric of American history.

Sarah Lockwood Winchester was one of the richest women in the world in 1880 after the death of her husband, William Wirt Winchester. She was the heiress of millions of dollars, fifty percent of the holdings of the Winchester Repeating Arms Company, and the Winchester family curse.

Oliver Winchester, a clothing manufacturer in New York City, bought a failing division of Smith & Wesson that focused on a newly patented arms in 1855. Winchester, with the help of the innovative engineer Benjamin Tyler Henry, redesigned the repeating rifle to astounding success. The riches were left to the lonely heiress plagued by the company's effect on the world.

Can't Buy Me Love

The couple was devestated when their newborn daughter died of marasmus in 1866. And when Oliver Winchester passed away, William stepped into his dad's shoes at the family business. However, he had only held the job for a few months when he lost a battle with tuberculosis and died in 1881. Sarah was now forty-one years old, broken hearted, and extremely wealthy. In the late 1880s, the average family income hovered around $500 per year. Sarah was pulling in about $1,000 per day! Because her husband left her everything, she had more than 700 shares of stock in addition to income from current sales. Sarah was up to her eyeballs in money. When William's mother died in 1898, Sarah inherited 2,000 more shares, which meant that she owned about fifty percent of the business. Sarah Winchester was all dressed up and had absolutely nowhere to go—even if she did have someplace, there was no one with whom she could share it.

She Sees Dead People

Sarah was not doing well after the death of her husband. Losing her daughter to a childhood disease fifteen years earlier had been a debilitating blow, but after her husband's passing, she was barely able to function. Fearing for her life, one of Sarah's close friends suggested she visit a psychic to see if she could contact her husband or daughter or both.

Sarah agreed to visit a Boston medium named Adam Coons, who wasted no time in telling her that William was trying to communicate with her, and the message wasn't good.

Apparently, William was desperate to tell Sarah that the family was cursed as a result of the invention of the repeating rifle. Native Americans, settlers, and soldiers all over the world were dead, largely due to the Winchester family. The spirits of these people were out for Sarah next, said William through the medium. The only way for her to prolong her life was to "head toward the setting sun," which meant, "move to California." The medium told her that once she got there, she would have to build a house where all those spirits could live happily together—but the house had to be built big and built often. Sarah was told that construction on the house could never cease, or the spirits would claim her and she would die. So Sarah packed up and left New Haven for California in 1884.

Teddy Roosevelt praised the Winchester repeating rifle during his hunting expeditions out West.

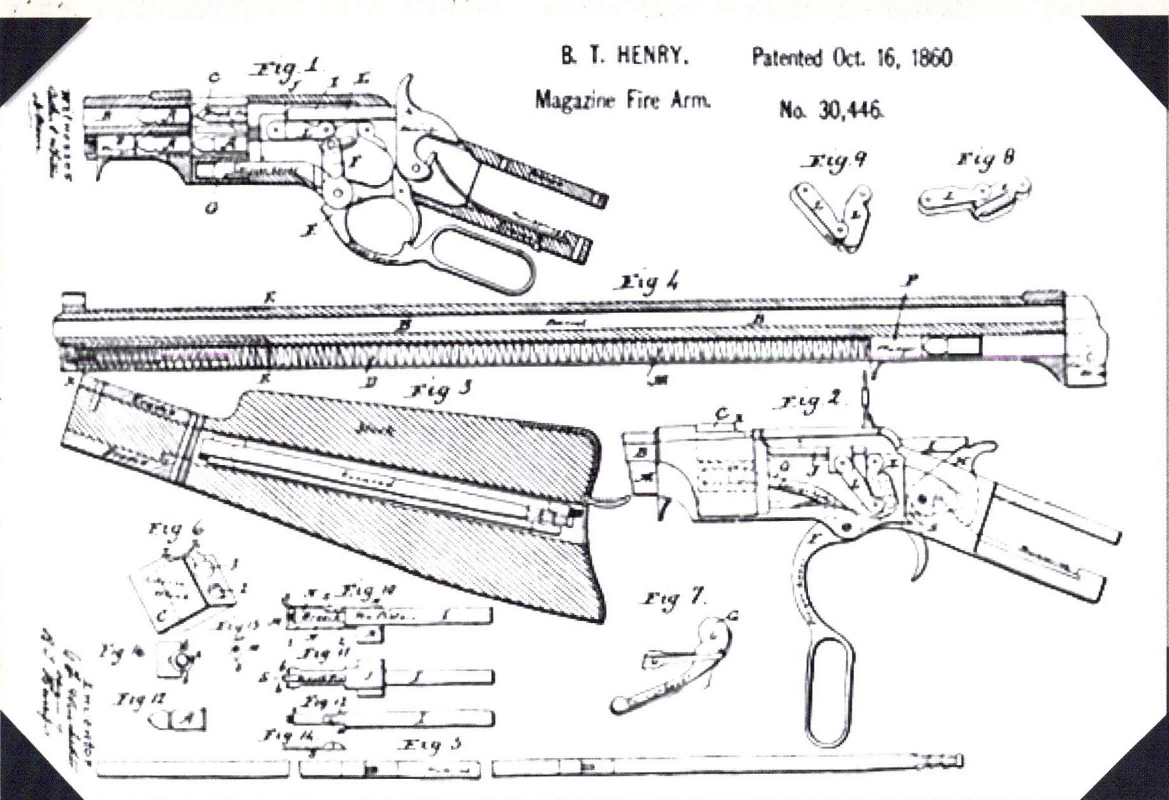

The 1860 patent drawing of the original repeating "Henry" rifle.

Sarah and many others claimed the house was haunted by the souls of those who died in the crosshairs of the Winchester rifle, the "Gun That Won the West."

Now That's a House

Sarah bought an eight-room farmhouse on the outskirts of the burgeoning town of San José, on the southern end of San Francisco Bay. Legend has it that she hired more than twenty workmen and a foreman and kept them working twenty-four hours a day, 365 days a year. To ensure that they would keep quiet about what they were doing—and not leave because the house was more than a little weird—she paid them a whopping $3 per day—more than twice the going rate of the time.

The workmen took the money and built as their client wished, though it made no sense whatsoever. Sarah was not an architect, but she gave the orders for the house's design. Sarah's odd requests, the constant construction, and an endless stream of money resulted in a rather unusual abode—stairs lead to ceilings, windows open into brick walls, and some rooms have no doors. There are also Tiffany windows all over the place, many containing the number thirteen, with which Sarah was obsessed. There are spiderweb-paned windows, which, although lovely, didn't do much to dispel rumors that Sarah was preoccupied with death and the occult.

The house kept on growing, all because the spirits were supposedly "advising" Sarah. Chimneys were built and never used. There were so many rooms that counting them was pointless. Reportedly, one stairway in the house went up seven steps and down eleven, and one of the linen closets is bigger than most three-bedroom apartments.

Very few people ever saw the lady of the house. When she shopped in town, merchants came to her car, as she rarely stepped out. Rumors were rampant in San Jose: Who was this crazy lady? Was the house haunted by spirits or just the energy of the aggrieved widow who lived there? Would the hammers ever stop banging? The workers knew how weird the house was, but no one knew for sure what went on inside Sarah's head.

Sarah's will was divided into exactly thirteen parts and was signed thirteen times. Her belongings, everything from ornate furniture to chandeliers, were auctioned off. It took six weeks to remove everything from the house.

The house at the time of Sarah's passing covered several acres and had more than 10,000 window panes, 160 rooms, 467 doorways, 47 fireplaces, 40 stairways, and 6 kitchens.

Sarah Winchester's bedroom. In 1922, Sarah Winchester died in her sleep, and the construction finally ceased after thirty-eight years. In her will, Sarah left huge chunks of her estate to nieces, nephews, and loyal employees.

The Curse Continues

With so many people going in and out of the house over the years, it's not surprising that there are tales of "strange happenings" in the Winchester mansion. People have claimed that they've heard and seen banging doors, mysterious voices, cold spots, moving lights, doorknobs that turn by themselves, and more than a few say that Sarah herself still roams the many rooms. Psychics who have visited the house solemnly swear that it is indeed haunted.

This can't be proven, of course, but it doesn't stop the claims, and it didn't stop the lady of the house from undertaking one of the world's most incredible construction projects.

The USS *Hornet*:

The Spirits of World War II Live On (Alameda, California)

The USS *Hornet* is a floating piece of history. This World War II-era aircraft carrier is as long as three football fields, and in her heyday, she housed a hospital, a tailor shop, a cobbler shop, three barbershops, and seven galleys. The recipient of nine battle stars for military service, the *Hornet* could carry 3,500 sailors. During World War II, her pilots destroyed 1,410 Japanese aircrafts and almost 1.3 tons of enemy cargo. But in her twenty-seven years of service, the *Hornet* saw 300 deaths from battles, accidents, and suicides; in fact, this ship is believed to hold the Navy record for the most suicides. If that isn't enough to produce a ghost or two, what is?

The USS *Hornet* served in WWII and the Vietnam War. It also played a part in NASA's Apollo program, recovering the astronauts of the *Apollo 11* and *Apollo 12* missions returning from the moon.

It's a Strange, Strange World

Considered one of the most haunted ships in history, the USS *Hornet* now sits docked at the Alameda Naval Air Station in California. Since completing a storied military career, the ship has become a naval museum—which happens to be full of ghosts.

Since the *Hornet*'s arrival in Alameda, tourists and staff members have noticed some very strange phenomena aboard the old ship. In fact, several websites are devoted to reporting strange happenings on the *Hornet*, all of which are noted by regular people who just happen to experience them. Many witnesses were self-proclaimed skeptics who are now believers.

The paranormal activity on the USS *Hornet* includes unusual noises, items that come up missing, and apparitions. Psychics and ghost hunters who have investigated the abnormal occurrences there agree that the ship's spirits are probably the souls of departed sailors who died abruptly. Perhaps they're still trying to carry out their final orders.

Many people report feeling that someone touched or grabbed them when no one else was in sight. There's no need to be afraid, though, because almost all accounts describe friendly spirits. In fact, many of the ghosts—which are primarily men—are quite the pranksters.

Sailors firing anti-aircraft guns on February 16, 1945, as the carrier's planes raided Tokyo.

And oddly, not all of them seem to be naval men: Members of other branches of the military—dressed in their respective uniforms—have also been spotted onboard.

No place is off limits to these free spirits. Those who have seen the ghostly figures on the ship say they are so real-looking that they blend in with the living. They appear dressed in uniform, patrolling the hallways and performing their shipboard duties. They've also been spotted on decks, climbing ladders, in bathrooms, and in the Combat Information Center. Toilets mysteriously flush by themselves, lights turn on and off on their own, and men are heard talking in areas where no one else appears to be present.

The Spirits of World War II

The steam room is one of the most haunted sections of the USS *Hornet,* probably because it was one of the most dangerous areas of the ship. One sailor who died in the steam room is thought to remain there. Some say that because he died so quickly, he doesn't realize that he's dead.

Not all the ghosts on the USS *Hornet* are American. One spirit that has appeared to many visitors is that of a Japanese pilot who was a prisoner of war on board the ship during World War II; he allegedly went mad in the small cell in which he was kept. He still inhabits that room—and he's still trying to get out.

The *Hornet* damaged after a typhoon.

Another ghost that has been seen on the ship quite often is that of Admiral Joseph "Jocko" Clark, who served as the vessel's commander during World War II. After calling the *Hornet* home for so many years, it seems that his spirit may have sought out the place where he felt most at home. Even decades after his passing, he's still married to the sea.

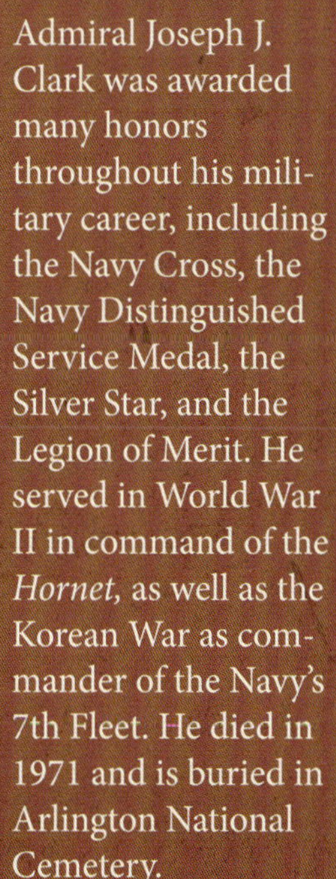

Admiral Joseph J. Clark was awarded many honors throughout his military career, including the Navy Cross, the Navy Distinguished Service Medal, the Silver Star, and the Legion of Merit. He served in World War II in command of the *Hornet,* as well as the Korean War as commander of the Navy's 7th Fleet. He died in 1971 and is buried in Arlington National Cemetery.

The Ghosts of Pike Place Market (Seattle, Washington)

Where Shopping Can Be a Spiritual Experience

Pike Place Market, which opened in August 1907, is one of the oldest farmers' markets in the United States. On its first day in business, more than 10,000 shoppers besieged the eight farmers who had brought their wares to Seattle's waterfront. By year's end, the market's first building was open, and it hasn't looked back since. Perhaps that's a good thing, because looking back might well reveal something else besides shoppers: ghosts.

One of the market's most frequent phantom visitors is Princess Angeline, the daughter of Chief Seattle, who was a leader of the tribes that lived in the area before the arrival of white settlers. By the late 1850s, many Native Americans had left the area due to the terms of a treaty between the tribes and the U.S. government. But Angeline stayed in Seattle and was a familiar figure along the waterfront. She became a local celebrity and was frequently photographed later in life.

Angeline died in 1896 at age eighty-five. So when Pike Place Market was built on the site of her former home, it was like sending out an open invitation for her to hang around for a while, and Angeline has apparently accepted the offer. Her apparition has been spotted at many different locations in the market, but she seems particularly fond of a wooden column on the lower level. Abnormally cold air is said to surround this column, and photographs of it reputedly show things that aren't apparent to the naked eye.

With her braided gray hair, slow way of moving, and habit of browsing, Angeline's ghost easily passes for an elderly shopper. She has often fooled people, who react to her as if she's a fellow consumer until she startles them by vanishing right before their eyes. Sometimes, Angeline even treats folks to a light show, changing from a glowing white figure to blue, lavender, or pink.

Princess Angeline, or Kikisoblu, daughter of the namesake of Seattle, Chief Seattle, was born on Rainier Beach in Seattle in 1820. She died in 1896 and is buried in Lake View Cemetery in the Capitol Hill neighborhood of Seattle.

You're Never Alone at Pike Place Market

While Angeline does her best to make as many ghostly appearances at the market as possible, she's not the only spectral spectacle at Pike Place. Workers have heard disembodied lullabies drifting through the air late at night after the market is closed; allegedly, they come from the ghost of a heavyset female barber who used to softly sing her customers to sleep and then pick their pockets while they snoozed. Unfortunately, she was not as good at walking as singing, and one day she fell through a weak floor to her death. Nevertheless, her ethereal song continues, which seems to contradict the saying, "It ain't over until the fat lady sings."

Another spirit that calls Pike Place home is Arthur Goodwin, the market's director from 1918 to 1941. Ever the workaholic, Arthur's silhouette can often be seen looking down at the market from his former office on the upper floor, still keeping an eye on the business.

What's more, a small spectral boy is seen in a craft shop that sells beads. He's been known to open and shut the cash register and tug at sleeves to get attention. At one point during renovations to the store, a small cache of beads was discovered in a wall; it's believed that the ghostly boy was stashing beads there to play with later, as kids often do.

Some more temperamental ghosts have been heard arguing inside the walk-in freezer of a Pike Place deli. A few deli employees simply refuse to go into the freezer because they're afraid of being drawn into whatever disagreement these spirits have with each other.

Princess Angeline refused to leave the city limits of Seattle as was required of all Duwamish Indians by the 1855 Treaty of Point Elliot. Instead, she continued to live in her cottage on Western Ave. in between Pike and Pine Streets, today's location of Seattle's Pike Place Market.

The Ghosts of Yosemite National Park (Tuolumne County, California)

The Creepy Canyon

Back in the 19th century, the ability of Native Americans to marshal the wrath of the spirit world was dismissed as superstitious mumbo-jumbo. That's unfortunate, because if it had been taken more seriously, people might have feared the consequences of the words of Chief Tenaya of the Ahwahneechee tribe. In 1851, when white settlers were trying to force his people out of the Yosemite Valley in what is now Yosemite National Park, Chief Tenaya put a curse on the land.

It turns out that the chief wasn't just making an idle gesture. In the park's Tenaya Canyon, a disproportionate number of tragic incidents have occurred: Visitors to the area have become lost, drowned, fallen to their deaths, and died of hypothermia. Once, a pilot who was looking for an injured hiker was purportedly overcome by vertigo and nearly flew his chopper into the side of the canyon. Not even Yosemite champion John Muir was spared from the alleged curse: During his first visit to the canyon, Muir fell and was knocked unconscious while scaling cliffs in "the Bermuda Triangle of Yosemite," as Tenaya Canyon is sometimes called.

Apparently, Tenaya is not above more forceful demonstrations to exact his revenge. In 1996, a Native American who had been born in the park and had spent his entire life working there as a maintenance technician was preparing to retire. At that time, park officials were told that Ahwahneechee legend warned that the last Yosemite-born Indian's departure from the park would bring disaster. But in late December 1996, with their heads firmly buried in the sand, park officials let the man retire and leave the confines of the park.

A few days later, on January 1, a freak storm resulted in a flood that caused $178 million in damage to the park. Some months later (and possibly with a nervous nod to Tenaya), park officials agreed to establish a traditional Native American village in Yosemite Valley.

Sometimes Tenaya steps aside and allows others to do the supernatural heavy lifting at Yosemite. Visitors to the park have reported seeing and even speaking with Native American apparitions. Legends tell of a ghost boy that inhabits the waters of Grouse Lake; he reportedly likes to grab the legs of swimmers and pull them underneath the water. It is also said that an evil spirit wind inhabits Bridalveil Fall and that this wind is always ready to send an unsuspecting soul plummeting into the falls to his or her death.

Archeological finds in the Yosemite Valley reveal that humans have inhabited the area for the past 3,000 years, while humans began to visit the area nearly 8,000 to 10,000 years ago.

Let alone the curse Chief Tenaya invoked on the area, Tenaya Canyon is notoriously tough to traverse. It has no maintained foot trails and is extremely dangerous in the spring and summer because of high water. Numerous accidents, mysterious deaths, and disappearances have occurred in the canyon.

The Stoneman Bridge was originally a wooden structure from 1887 to 1918 before it was rebuilt as a reinforced concrete girder bridge with concrete and granite abutments. The ghostly couple that has been seen lingering around the bridge supposedly died while swimming in 2005.

A Ghostly Group

Some standard hauntings round out the supernatural smorgasbord at Yosemite. According to legend, a lonely camper once hung himself in his tent; late at night, his body can supposedly still be seen slowly swinging forlornly from the tent frame. Also, a young couple who drowned near Stoneman Bridge has been seen on or near the span on many occasions.

Yosemite's Ahwahnee Hotel is the park's own "Apparition Inn." The building was used as a convalescent home for soldiers during World War II, and it is believed that many of its ghosts are the spirits of those troops. The hotel's former operator, Mary Curry Tresidder, lived in the building for many years until she died in the 1960s, and apparently, she isn't letting a little thing like death force her to check out: She's still seen on the sixth floor, perhaps making certain that the guests are comfortable.

However, for sheer spiritual star power, nothing can top the phantom rocking chair that appears from time to time on the third floor. In 1962, President John F. Kennedy stayed in a third-floor suite, and the hotel placed a rocking chair in the room for his comfort. The chair was removed after Kennedy left; however, since his assassination in 1963, housekeepers have witnessed a rocking chair slowly swaying back and forth in the room in which he stayed. When they glance away from the chair, it disappears.

If it is indeed JFK still enjoying the pleasures of Yosemite, he's obviously not alone. From Native Americans to presidents to plain folks, Yosemite is a difficult place to leave for both the living and the dead.

Architect Gilbert Stanley Underwood's concept of the Ahwahnee Hotel presented the hotel in a much grander scale than what was actually built.

The Ghosts of the *Titanic* Exhibit (Various)

On April 14, 1912, the supposedly unsinkable RMS *Titanic* struck an iceberg in the North Atlantic, and by the end of the next day, approximately 1,500 souls lay in a cold, watery grave. Nestled deep in frigid waters, their resting place remained undisturbed until the wreck was discovered on the ocean floor in 1985. Two years later, salvage divers began to recover artifacts from the wreck. Since then, about 5,900 items have been taken from the site. Many of these objects are included in *Titanic*: The Artifact Exhibition, which has traveled the world since the early 1990s—and a few ghosts have gone along for the ride. A permanent *Titanic* museum is also haunted by the past.

Haunting Atlanta

While taking in the traveling exhibit at the Georgia Aquarium in Atlanta, a visitor initially attributed a sense of being watched and feelings of overwhelming sadness to the items on display. One volunteer who worked at the exhibit said she sensed that lost souls were embedded in the artifacts; she also felt a hand moving over her head and touching her hair. And a four-year-old boy repeatedly asked his mother and grandmother about a lady that he saw in a display case, which—to the adults—held only a dress and a love seat. Another visitor saw a man in a black-and-white suit who seemed out of place amongst the other, more casually dressed people; later, when she felt as if she was being watched, the visitor turned around to see the man in the suit staring at her.

In 2008, when a paranormal investigation team visited the exhibit, its members witnessed shadowy figures and picked up the voices of spirits on audio recordings. The team concluded that at least three ghosts are attached to the exhibit—those of an older gentleman, an elderly woman, and a young crew member.

Jason Hawes and Grant Wilson and their team from The Atlantic Paranormal Society (TAPS) also conducted an investigation of the exhibit; their results aired on a 2009 episode of *Ghost Hunters*. Their findings were similar to those compiled by other paranormal research groups. In the Iceberg Exhibit (which contains a replica of an iceberg to give visitors a sense of what one feels like), Hawes and Wilson detected a moving cold spot that seemed to be about four to five feet tall and one to two feet wide. Hawes also felt something tug on his shirt. While in the Artifacts Exhibit, both investigators saw a shadowy figure walk into another room, and Hawes felt an unseen hand touch his shoulder. Before they left the room, Hawes asked the spirit to knock on the wall if it wanted them to leave. They heard nothing, but their audio recorder captured an EVP (electronic voice phenomenon) that sounded like a man whispering, "No, please wait," or perhaps even, "Don't leave me." In the end, TAPS concluded that both intelligent and residual hauntings were present at the aquarium, which are likely associated with the exhibit.

The *Titanic* under construction in the gantry of shipbuilders Harland & Wolff Heavy Industries in Belfast, Ireland.

The *Titanic* undergoing sea trials outside of Belfast, Ireland, on April 2, 1912.

At the Southhampton docks moments before its maiden departure.

The RMS *Titanic* leaving Southhampton, England, on its maiden voyage on April 10, 1912, five days before meeting its tragic fate in the North Atlantic.

Rocking New York City

When the exhibit traveled to New York City, motion-activated security cameras clicked on every night at 3 a.m., even though no living being was present. And one visitor said that as she and her cousin walked through a small hallway, they experienced a rocking sensation, as if they were actually on a ship. They asked an employee if this was some sort of special effect; it was not, but the employee reported that many other people had asked the same question.

The *Titanic* in Cork Harbour, Ireland, one day after its maiden departure.

Chilling St. Paul

When the artifacts visited St. Paul, Minnesota, one visitor left the Iceberg Exhibit because she suddenly felt dizzy. Then, she felt a hand touching her shoulder, even though no one else was around. Her shoulder felt cold and then hot, as if she had frostbite. A few minutes later, a red mark appeared on her shoulder. Another person reported similar sensations when leaving the Iceberg Exhibit, including dizziness, shoulder taps, and the queasy sensation of being rocked.

Ghosts in Branson

Even a permanent *Titanic* museum seems to be haunted. The *Titanic* museum attraction in Branson, Missouri (and its sister site in Pigeon Forge, Tennessee), is said to be teeming with ghosts. This re-creation of the legendary ship displays approximately 400 artifacts from the actual *Titanic*—and is thought to be home to at least one ghost-child. Members of the cleaning staff have found child-size fingerprints on the glass separating the Promenade Deck and the Bridge; given that many children visit the museum, this is not unusual. However, the prints reappear after the glass is cleaned when the museum is closed. Even stranger, one museum employee photographed a wet footprint in the shape of a child's bare foot.

Ghosts have also been spotted in other parts of the ship: A man in formal wear has been seen at the top of the Grande Staircase; a gowned figure glides around the First Class Dining Salon and emerges from the area carrying her belongings; and although the museum has a no smoking policy, both staffers and visitors have smelled cigar smoke around the Grande Staircase on numerous occasions.

To determine once and for all if ghosts from the *Titanic* haunt the museum, the owners invited two different teams of paranormal investigators to conduct research overnight. Both teams found high psychic-energy levels that became higher when staff members asked the spirits questions. As museum staffers communicated with two passengers who died on the ship—Robert Douglas Spedden and Mr. Asplund—one staff member became weak and nauseous.

Final Attachments

When the exhibit visited Athens, Greece, employees heard English-speaking voices in the galleries after hours. And in Monterrey, Mexico, several people commented on a man who they described as a "character actor" dressed in a black suit that would have been fashionable in 1912. However, the exhibit did not employ any re-enactors.

It makes sense that *Titanic*'s victims would follow the items that they knew in life and rested with in death for many decades. The artifacts will continue to travel the world as long as there is interest in them, but hopefully, the spirits will eventually separate themselves from their earthly belongings and finally rest in peace.

A photo taken on the morning of April 15, 1912, hours after the sinking of the *Titanic*, of what is believed to be the iceberg that damaged and separated the below-waterline seams of the ship's starboard hull.

Survivors of the accident photographed from the *Carpathia*, the vessel nearest to the *Titanic* that responded to the distress calls. The *Carpathia* steamed through the night at full speed and at considerable risk to come to the rescue, maneuvering around icebergs en route to the crash site.

The Mansfield Reformatory
(Mansfield, Ohio)

As you turn onto Reformatory Road in Mansfield, Ohio, you can't help but gasp as you gaze upon the immense castlelike structure that looms before you.

From Camp to Castle

During the Civil War, the property on which the Mansfield Reformatory now stands was the site of Camp Mordecai Bartley. After the war, the decision was made to construct a reformatory there that would function as a sort of "middle ground" for first-time offenders, allowing only hardened criminals and repeat offenders to be sent to the Ohio Penitentiary in Columbus. But the Mansfield Reformatory would be no ordinary structure—it would be an imposing edifice designed to strike fear into the heart of any prisoner forced to enter its massive gates.

In the 1880s, architect Levi T. Scofield began designing the reformatory. The entire front portion would house the warden, his family, and the administrative offices; the rear portion would contain the massive six-tier cellblock, which would be the tallest freestanding cellblock in the world.

Incredibly, when the Mansfield Reformatory finally opened in September 1896, the 150 inmates transferred there entered a building that still wasn't complete. In fact, the prisoners themselves were responsible for finishing the construction, a task that included completing a giant wall surrounding the main building. The structure would not be fully finished until 1910.

The reformatory opened on September 15, 1896, to the first 150 inmates who were immediately put to work on finishing the reformatory's sewer system and the stone wall that surrounded the complex.

Cramped Quarters and Violence

It doesn't seem possible that such a massive building could become overcrowded, but that's exactly what happened: By 1930, the reformatory was already well over capacity. In fact, inmates were often sleeping three or four to a cell that was designed to fit only two.

The cramped quarters may have been one reason why prisoners at the Mansfield Reformatory were so aggressive. Considering the fact that the facility did not house hardened criminals, the amount of violence that took place there is staggering. A riot in 1957 involved more than 100 inmates. There were also a few instances in which one inmate killed another. Several prisoners couldn't take the living conditions and committed suicide, including one man who set himself on fire. Eventually, word of the horrible conditions reached the public, and in the early 1980s, officials declared the Mansfield Reformatory unfit to continue functioning as a prison; it would be another ten years before the facility was actually shut down.

Haunted by the Past

One of the most enduring ghost stories associated with the Mansfield Reformatory centers on Warden Arthur L. Glattke and his wife, Helen. In 1950, Helen was getting ready for Sunday mass when she went into a closet in the warden's quarters to retrieve a box from a high shelf. As she grabbed the box, she bumped a revolver that Arthur had hidden in the closet; the gun went off and wounded her. She was rushed to the hospital, but she died several days later of pneumonia while recovering from her injury.

On February 10, 1959, Arthur was working in his office when he suffered a fatal heart attack. Almost immediately, rumors began to suggest that Helen's death had not been an accident, but rather that Arthur had killed her and made it look like an accident. Further, it was said that Arthur's heart attack was the result of Helen's ghost exacting its revenge. It's a creepy story, but it can't be proven. In fact, by all accounts, the couple truly loved each other. Perhaps that's why when people see the ghosts of the couple, they appear happy as they walk up and down the hallways of the warden's quarters.

Investigating the Reformatory

While the Mansfield Reformatory had been featured on numerous television shows such as *Scariest Places on Earth*, it wasn't until The Atlantic Paranormal Society (TAPS) visited in 2005 for *Ghost Hunters* that people everywhere got a look at a paranormal investigation inside the prison's walls.

During that investigation, TAPS members heard strange footsteps echoing throughout the prison; they also managed to videotape unexplained lights at the far end of the hallway in solitary confinement. But the most intriguing part of the evening came when investigators Dustin Pari and Dave Tango were walking on the second floor of the East Cellblock. The duo heard strange noises coming from one of the cells, but when they were unable to find the source of the sounds, they marked an *X* outside the cell so they could find it later. About an hour later, investigators Jason Hawes and Grant Wilson were in the same area when Hawes thought that he saw something moving inside the cell marked with an *X*, and Wilson believed he heard something there. However, upon investigating the cell, it appeared to be empty.

The East Cellblock, pictured here, is the largest free standing steel cellblock in the world at six tiers high.

The Camp Chase
Confederate Cemetery (Columbus, Ohio)

Established in May 1861, Camp Chase served as a prison for Confederate officers during the Civil War. However, as the number of Confederate POWs grew, the prison could not be quite so selective. As 1863 dawned, Camp Chase held approximately 8,000 men of every rank.

The sheer number of prisoners soon overwhelmed Camp Chase. Men were forced to share bunks, and shortages of food, clothing, medicine, and other necessities were common. Under those conditions, the prisoners were vulnerable to disease and malnutrition, which led to many deaths—500 in one particular month alone, due to an outbreak of smallpox. Eventually, a cemetery was established at the camp to handle the large number of bodies.

Although Camp Chase was closed shortly after the war, the cemetery remains. Today, it contains the graves of more than 2,100 Confederate soldiers. Although restless spirits are commonly found where miserable deaths occurred, just one ghost is known to call Camp Chase its "home haunt": the famous Lady in Gray. Dressed in a flowing gray dress with a veil hiding her face, she is often seen standing and sobbing over Benjamin F. Allen's grave. At other times, she can be found weeping at the grave of an unidentified soldier. Occasionally, she leaves flowers on the tombstones.

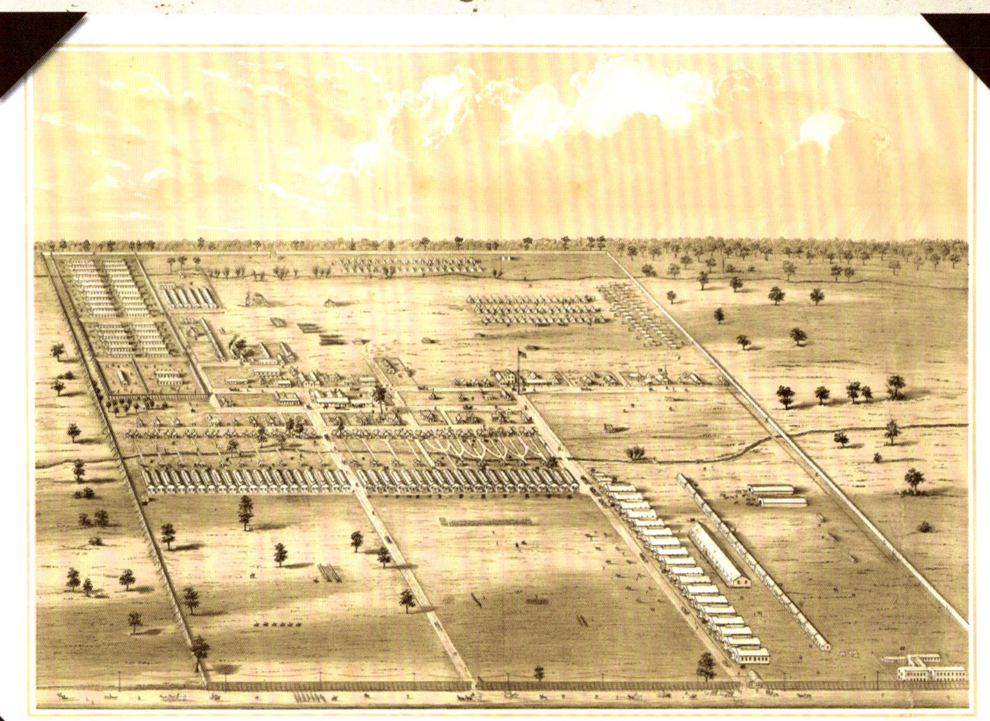

Between the Civil War's onset and terminus (1861–1865), nearly 150,000 Union soldiers and 25,000 Confederate prisoners passed through Camp Chase. By 1865, nearly 9,400 Confederates were imprisoned at the camp and 2,200 Confederates interred in the cemetery.

The Lady in Gray has also been spotted walking among the many gravestones in the cemetery; she's even been observed passing right through the locked cemetery gates. No one knows who she was in life, but some speculate that she was Allen's wife. However, her attention to the grave of the unknown soldier baffles researchers. One thing seems certain, though: As long as the Camp Chase Confederate Cemetery exists, the Lady in Gray will watch over it.

The Haunting of Hull House (Chicago, Illinois)

In 1856, wealthy businessman Charles J. Hull constructed a mansion at Halsted and Polk streets on Chicago's near west side, at the time one of the most fashionable sections of the city. But the Great Fire of 1871 sent wealthy Chicagoans to other parts of the city, and the near west side began to attract a large population of Italian, Greek, and Jewish immigrants. It became one of the most dangerous slums in the city, and by the 1880s, Hull House was surrounded by factories, bordellos, taverns, and rundown tenement houses. In 1889, it was exactly the sort of neighborhood that Jane Addams was seeking.

Jane Addams's Hull House

Born into an affluent family in 1860, Jane Addams knew nothing of poverty as a child. But when her father died, she sank into a deep depression, so she traveled to Europe to escape from her grief. It was there, in the slums of London, that she realized her life's calling.

Jane and Ellen Gates Starr, her friend and traveling companion, volunteered with the poor at Toynbee Hall, a settlement house in the poverty-stricken Whitechapel neighborhood. There, affluent students like Jane and Ellen worked alongside the most undesirable members of British society, offering food, education, and medical care while lobbying for social reform and improved standards of living for the poor. Jane was invigorated by her work at Toynbee Hall and soon made plans to start a similar project in Chicago.

By the time Addams came to the west side with the intention of starting a settlement house, the crowded neighborhood was teeming with poverty, crime, and prostitution. Numerous brothels, saloons, and dope dealers victimized the refugees and immigrants who came to America with little money and were often unable to speak English. It was to these people that Jane Addams became the "voice of humanity."

Impressed by Jane's plans for a settlement house, Helen Culver, Charles Hull's niece, offered the mansion to Addams with a rent-free lease. Addams and Starr converted the mansion into a safe and comfortable place that offered food, shelter, and education for the impoverished. As the operation increased in popularity, twelve more buildings were added, until eventually Hull House spread out over an entire city block.

When Jane Addams died in 1935, the Hull House Association took over the property and continued her efforts until the 1960s, when the University of Illinois at Chicago bought the property. Hull House was named a historic site, but the additional buildings around the mansion were torn down. And though much has changed, some things remain the same—such as the resident ghosts of Hull House, including a spirit that Jane Addams herself witnessed on numerous occasions!

The Ghost of Mrs. Hull

Charles Hull's wife had died of natural causes in a second-floor bedroom of the mansion several years before Jane Addams took up residence in the home. Addams occupied Mrs. Hull's former bedroom and was awakened by the sound of footsteps pacing back and forth. When Ellen confessed that she'd heard the same noises, too, Addams moved to another bedroom.

Jane, Ellen, and other staff members were not the only ones to witness the strange occurrences in the house. Visitors and overnight guests experienced Mrs. Hull's presence, too. Author Helen Campbell claimed to see a ghostly woman standing next to her bed when she spent the night in the haunted room. When she turned on a light, the apparition disappeared.

In Jane Addams's autobiography, *Twenty Years at Hull House*, she stated that earlier tenants of the mansion believed that the attic was haunted, so they always left a bucket of water on the steps because they thought a ghost would not be able to pass it and descend to the lower floors.

Hull House operated several facilities by 1911, all of which were located in the immediate area of the original Hull Mansion. All of the buildings except for the dining hall and mansion were torn down in the 1960s for the construction of the University of Illinois, Chicago. The dining hall and mansion are now a part of the campus's Jane Addam's Hull-House Museum. Pictured here is Smith Hall which was located on the southwest corner of Polk and Halsted Streets.

The "Devil Baby"

By 1913, rumors were circulating that Hull House was the refuge of a "Devil Baby," and the organization's reputation as a great example of social reform was tarnished. According to the widely spread story, this horribly deformed child was the son of a Catholic woman whose husband was an atheist. When the young woman hung a picture of the Virgin Mary in her home, her husband angrily tore it down, screaming that he would rather have the devil himself in his home than a picture of the Virgin Mary. He soon got his wish!

When his wife became pregnant a short time later, she was carrying the "Devil Baby" in her womb. Allegedly, the baby was born with pointed ears, horns, and a tail. Unable to endure the insults and tormenting by his neighbors, the husband abandoned the child at Hull House.

The baby, who was born with the ability to speak both English and Latin, continued to be a nuisance while at Hull House. While being baptized, he purportedly leapt from the priest's arms and began dancing, laughing, and singing. Unable to make the child behave, Jane had him locked away in the attic of Hull House, safe from prying eyes.

Looking east on Polk Street toward Halsted Street, this picture shows us from right to left the Boy's Club Building, Bowen Hall, the gymansium, the theater, and Smith Hall.

Hauntings Today

What remains of Hull House today is located on Halsted Street and is open as a historical site. The University of Illinois at Chicago built its campus around the mansion in the 1960s, leaving no trace of the old neighborhood that once existed. The crumbling tenements, brothels, and saloons have been replaced by loft apartments, parking lots, and ethnic restaurants.

Today, Hull House remains an attraction for tourists, history buffs, and ghost enthusiasts. It is not uncommon for motion sensors to be triggered, even when no one is at the house. Officers report that no other building on campus gets as many false alarm calls as Hull House. They have also answered calls about people looking out of the windows after the museum is closed, but they have never found anyone in the place after hours.

One incident that remains unexplained occurred when a front window of the house was shattered a few years ago. Officers rushed to the scene but found no one there. The strange thing was that the window appeared to be broken from inside the house, yet police found no evidence of a break-in and no sign that anyone had been in the house at all.

Visitors who have come to Hull House during the evening hours often report strange occurrences. There are many claims of lights turning on and off, shadowy figures seen moving inside, and shutters that open and close by themselves.

There are many possible suspects in the haunting of this house, including the ghost of Mrs. Hull, the lingering spirit of one of the poor people that Jane Addams tried to save, and, of course, the "Devil Baby," whose spirit may still be trapped in the mansion's attic. It might be any one of these restless spirits, or perhaps all of them. It's no surprise that many call Hull House the most haunted house in Chicago!

A Haunting on Chicago's Magnificent Mile (Chicago, Illinois)

The Chicago Water Tower stands more than 150 feet tall along the world-famous Magnificent Mile—one of the city's most popular tourist attractions. However, many visitors don't realize that the site is haunted by a hero who died there during the Great Chicago Fire of 1871.

Mrs. O'Leary Lit a Lantern in the Shed

On the evening of October 8, 1871, the Great Chicago Fire began behind the O'Leary home. Contrary to popular belief, the fire was not started by a cow kicking over a lantern. Nevertheless, the flames spread quickly from the O'Leary barn. When the smoke cleared a couple of days later, charred buildings and ashes littered the city. Approximately 300 people died in the fire, but the heat was so intense that only 125 bodies were recovered. One of those bodies was a suicide victim found inside the Chicago Water Tower.

A Hero's Last Resort?

According to legend, a lone fireman remained steadfast at the water-pumping station in Chicago's Streeterville neighborhood trying to save as many homes as possible. But as the flames closed in around him, he realized it was a losing battle. With his back to the Chicago Water Tower, there was no place to run. As the fire edged closer, the brave fireman considered his options. Apparently, a slow death by fire seemed more frightening than a quicker end by his own hand. So the story goes that the fireman climbed the stairs inside the water tower, strung a rope from a beam near the top of the structure, and, in a moment of desperation, looped the rope around his neck and jumped to his death.

The fire was ostensibly started by Mrs. O'Leary's cow and lasted for two days in October of 1871. The Chicago River, which normally would have worked as a firebreak, fueled the fire with its lumber and coal yards around its banks.

The Solitary Ghost

The heat of the fire did not destroy the Chicago Water Tower, but it did scorch everything inside. The heroic fireman's identity was never known, but his spirit lingers. Hundreds of people have seen the sad figure of the hanging man and smelled a suggestion of smoke inside the tower, especially on October nights around the anniversary of the tragedy. From outside the historic structure, some people see a pale man staring down at them from a window near the top of the tower. His expression is sad and resigned, and he seems to look right through those on the ground. Other visitors have reported an eerie, sorrowful whistling that seems to come from inside the structure. It echoes through the tower, and then it stops abruptly. However, most people who've seen the Water Tower ghost describe him with a rope around his neck, swinging and turning slowly. His face is twisted and as if flames are just beneath him. The ghost appears so real that many witnesses have called police to report a suicide. But responding officers, who have often seen the apparition themselves, know that he's a ghost…and a reminder of valor during a tragic fire more than a century ago.

The Destruction after the Fire

The great Chicago Fire devastated the city of Chicago and its residents, leaving much of the downtown area completely destroyed with little left other than the stone skeletons of buildings.

The Great Chicago Fire raged at such high temperatures that it took several days after it ended before the remains were cool enough to be inspected.

The fire burned nearly 2,000 acres of land at 4 miles in length and $^{3}/_{4}$ of a mile in width. Nearly 73 miles of roads, 120 miles of sidewalks, 17,500 buildings, and 2,000 lampposts were destroyed in the fire, leaving 100,000 of Chicago's population of 300,000 homeless.

Lingering Spirits of the *Eastland* Disaster (Chicago, Illinois)

The *Eastland* was commissioned in 1902 and was plagued by problems from early on. A design flaw which made the steamer susceptible to heel, or tilt from one side to another, was realized after construction.

The city of Chicago has a dark history of disaster and death, with devastating fires, horrific accidents, and catastrophic events. One of the most tragic took place on July 24, 1915. On that overcast, summer afternoon, hundreds of people died in the Chicago River when the *Eastland* capsized just a few feet from the dock. This calamity left a ghostly impression on the Windy City that is still felt today.

Company Picnic Turns Tragic

July 24 was going to be a special day for thousands of Chicagoans. It was reserved for the annual summer picnic for employees of the Western Electric Company, which was to be held across Lake Michigan in Michigan City, Indiana. And although officials at the utility company had encouraged workers to bring along friends and relatives, they were surprised when more than 7,000 people arrived to be ferried across the lake on the five excursion boats chartered for the day. Three of the steamers—the *Theodore Roosevelt*, the *Petoskey*, and the *Eastland*—were docked on the Chicago River near Clark Street.

On this fateful morning, the *Eastland*, a steamer owned by the St. Joseph–Chicago Steamship Company, was filled to its limit. The boat had a reputation for top-heaviness and instability, and the new federal Seaman's Act, which was passed in 1915 as a result of the *Titanic* tragedy, required more lifeboats than previous regulations did. All of this resulted in the ship being even more unstable than it already was. In essence, it was a recipe for disaster.

Death and the *Eastland*

As passengers boarded the *Eastland*, she began listing back and forth. This had happened on the ship before, so the crew emptied the ballast compartments to provide more stability. As the boat was preparing to depart, some passengers went below deck, hoping to warm up on the cool, cloudy morning, but many on the overcrowded steamer jammed their way onto the deck to wave to onlookers on shore. The *Eastland* tilted once again, but this time more severely, and passengers began to panic. Moments later, the *Eastland* rolled to her side, coming to rest at the bottom of the river, only eighteen feet below the surface. One side of the boat's hull was actually above the water's surface in some spots.

A photo of the *Eastland* touring in 1911.

Passengers on deck were tossed into the river, splashing about in a mass of bodies. The overturned ship created a current that pulled some of the floundering swimmers to their doom, while many of the women's long dresses were snagged on the ship, tugging them down to the bottom.

Those inside were thrown to one side of the ship when it capsized. Heavy furniture onboard crushed some passengers and those who were not killed instantly drowned a few moments later when water rushed inside. A few managed to escape, but most of them didn't. Their bodies were later found trapped in a tangled heap on the lowest side of the *Eastland*.

Firefighters, rescue workers, and volunteers soon arrived and tried to help people escape through portholes. They also cut holes in the portion of the ship's hull that was above the water line. Approximately 1,660 passengers survived the disaster, but they still ended up in the river, and many courageous people from the wharf jumped in or threw life preservers as well as lines, boxes, and anything that floated into the water to the panicked and drowning passengers.

The bodies of those who perished in the tragedy were wrapped in sheets and placed on the *Theodore Roosevelt* or lined up along the docks. Marshall Field's and other large stores sent wagons to carry the dead to hospitals, funeral homes, and makeshift morgues, such as the Second Regiment Armory, where more than 200 bodies were sent.

In the end, 844 people died, many of them young women and children. Officially, no clear explanation was given for why the vessel capsized, and the St. Joseph–Chicago Steamship Company was not held accountable for the disaster.

Hauntings at Harpo Studios

At the time of the *Eastland* disaster, the only public building large enough to be used as a temporary morgue was the Second Regiment Armory, located on Chicago's near west side. The dead were laid out on the floor of the armory and assigned identification numbers. Chicagoans whose loved ones had perished in the disaster filed through the rows of bodies, searching for familiar faces, but in twenty-two cases, there was no one left to identify them. Those families were completely wiped out. The names of these victims were learned from neighbors who came searching for their friends. The weeping, crying, and moaning of the bereaved echoed off the walls of the armory for days.

The last body to be identified was Willie Novotny, a seven-year-old boy whose parents and older sister had also perished on the *Eastland*. When extended family members identified the boy nearly a week after the disaster took place, a chapter was closed on one of Chicago's most horrific events.

Jack Woodford, a witness to the disaster that day, wrote about the incident in his autobiography saying, "As I watched in disoriented stupefication a steamer large as an ocean liner slowly turned over on its side as though it were a whale going to take a nap. I didn't believe a huge steamer had done this before my eyes, lashed to a dock, in perfectly calm water, in excellent weather, with no explosion, no fire, nothing. I thought I had gone crazy."

As years passed, the armory building went through several incarnations, including a stable and a bowling alley, before Harpo Studios, the production company owned by talk-show maven Oprah Winfrey, purchased it. A number of *The Oprah Show*'s staff members, security guards, and maintenance workers claim that the studio is haunted by the spirits of those who tragically lost their lives on the *Eastland*. Many employees have experienced unexplained phenomena, including the sighting of a woman in a long gray dress who walks the corridors and then mysteriously vanishes into the wall. Some believe she is the spirit of a mourner who came to the armory looking for her family and left a bit of herself behind at a place where she felt her greatest sense of loss.

The woman in gray may not be alone in her spectral travels through the old armory. Staff members have also witnessed doors opening and closing on their own and heard people sobbing, whispering, and moaning, as well as phantom footsteps on the lobby's staircase. Those who have experienced these strange events believe that the tragedy of yesterday is still manifesting itself in the old armory building's present state.

After the ship was removed from the river, it was sold and converted into the warship USS *Wilmette*. The ship never saw any action but was used as a training ship during World War II. After the war, it was decommissioned and eventually scrapped in 1947.

Chicago River Ghosts

In the same way that the former armory seems to have been impressed with a ghostly recording of past events, the Chicago River seems haunted, too. For years, people walking on the Clark Street bridge have heard crying, moaning, and pleas for help coming from the river. Some have even witnessed the apparitions of victims helplessly splashing in the water. On several occasions, some witnesses have called the police for help. One man even jumped into the river to save what he thought was an actual person drowning. When he returned to the surface, he discovered that he was in the water alone. He had no explanation for what he'd seen, other than to admit that it might have been a ghost.

So it seems that the horror of the *Eastland* disaster has left an imprint on this spot and continues to replay itself over and over again, ensuring that the unfortunate victims from the *Eastland* will never truly be forgotten.

The *Eastland* disaster created an uproar in the media, including a scathing report by Carl Sandburg, who was known more as a journalist than a poet at the time. Sandburg put the blame on regulators who ignored safety issues and the company who ordered employees to show for a "staged picnic." Eventually, four of the steamship company's employees (including the president of the company) and the engineer and captian of the *Eastland* were indicted, but they never charged because the evidence was not strong enough to convict.

A Superior Haunting: The *Edmund Fitzgerald* (Lake Superior, Whitefish Point, Michigan)

The 729-foot-long *Edmund Fitzgerald* was considered as unsinkable as any steamer. At its christening in June 1958, it was the Great Lakes' largest and most expensive freighter. Its name honored Edmund Fitzgerald, the president of Northwestern Mutual Insurance Company of Milwaukee, who commissioned the boat.

The Last Launch

The weather was unseasonably pleasant the morning of November 9, 1975, so much so that the crew of twenty-nine men who set sail from Superior, Wisconsin, that day were unlikely to have been concerned about their routine trip to Zug Island on the Detroit River. But the captain, Ernest McSorley, knew a storm was in the forecast.

McSorley was a forty-four-year veteran of the lakes, had captained the *Fitzgerald* since 1972, and was thought to have been planning his retirement for the following year. He paid close attention to the gale warnings issued that afternoon, but no one suspected they would turn into what weather-watchers called a "once in a lifetime storm." However, when the weather report was upgraded to a full storm warning, McSorley changed course to follow a route safer than the normal shipping lanes, instead chugging closer to the Canadian shore.

Following the *Fitzgerald* in a sort of "buddy" system was another freighter, the *Arthur Anderson*. The two captains stayed in contact as they traveled together through winds measuring up to fifty knots (about fifty-eight miles per hour) with waves splashing twelve feet or higher. Around 1:00 p.m., McSorley advised Captain Cooper of the *Anderson* that the *Fitzgerald* was "rolling." By about 2:45 p.m., as the *Anderson* moved to avoid a dangerous shoal near Caribou Island, a crewman sighted the *Fitzgerald* about sixteen miles ahead, closer to the shoal than Cooper thought safe.

About 3:30 p.m., McSorley reported to Cooper that the *Fitzgerald* had sustained some minor damage and was beginning to list, or roll to one side. The ships were still sixteen to seventeen miles apart. At 4:10 p.m., with waves now lashing eighteen feet high, McSorley radioed that his ship had lost radar capability. The two ships stayed in radio contact until about 7:00 p.m. when the *Fitzgerald* crew told the Anderson they were "holding [their] own." After that, radio contact was lost and the *Fitzgerald* dropped off the radar. Around 8:30 p.m., Cooper told the Coast Guard at Sault Ste. Marie that the *Fitzgerald* appeared to be missing. The search was on.

Evidently, the *Fitzgerald* sank sometime after 7:10 p.m. on November 10, just seventeen miles from the shore of Whitefish Point, Michigan. Despite a massive search effort, it wasn't until November 14 that a navy flyer detected a magnetic anomaly that turned out to be the wreck of the *Fitzgerald*. The only other evidence of the disaster to surface was a handful of lifeboats, life jackets, and some oars, tools, and propane tanks. A robotic vehicle was used to thoroughly photograph the wreck in May 1976.

During the *Fitzgerald's* christening, a few incidents occurred that some saw as bad omens. As a crowd of more than 10,000 watched, it took Mrs. Fitzgerald three tries to shatter the bottle of champagne. Then, when the ship was released into the water, it hit the surface at the wrong angle, causing a wave to splatter the entire ceremonial area with lake water and knocking the ship into a nearby dock. One spectator died on the spot of a heart attack.

One Mysterious Body

One troubling aspect of the *Fitzgerald* tragedy was that no bodies were found. In most lakes or temperate waters, corpses rise to the surface as decomposition causes gases to form, which makes bodies float. But the Great Lakes are so cold that decomposition and the formation of these gases is inhibited, causing bodies to remain on the lake bottom. One explanation was that the crew had been contained in the ship's enclosed areas.

In 1994, a Michigan businessman named Frederick Shannon took a tugboat and a sixteen-foot submarine equipped with a full array of modern surveillance equipment to the site, hoping to produce a documentary about the ship. But his crew was surprised when they discovered a body near the bow of the wreck, which had settled into the lake bottom. The remains were covered by cork sections of a deteriorated canvas life vest and were photographed but not retrieved. However, there was nothing to conclusively prove that this body was associated with the *Fitzgerald*. Two French vessels were lost in the same region in 1918, and none of those bodies had been recovered either. A sailor lost from one of them could have been preserved by the lake's frigid water and heavy pressure.

What Sank the Mighty *Fitz*?

One popular theory is that the *Fitzgerald* ventured too close to the dangerous Six-Fathom Shoal near Caribou Island and scraped over it, damaging the hull. Another is that the ship's hatch covers were either faulty or improperly clamped, which allowed water infiltration. Wave height may also have played its part, with the storm producing a series of gargantuan swells known as the "Three Sisters"—a trio of lightning-fast waves that pound a vessel with a one-two-three punch—the first washes over the deck, the second hits the deck again so fast that the first has not had time to clear itself, and the third quickly adds another heavy wash, piling thousands of gallons of water on the ship at once. Few ships have the ability to remain afloat under such an onslaught.

Spirits of the Lake

Author Hugh E. Bishop says that since the mighty *Fitz* went down, sailors have claimed to see a ghostly ship in the vicinity of the sinking. The captain of a Coast Guard cutter, the *Woodrush*, was on duty near the *Fitzgerald* site in 1976 and spent a night stuck in shifting ice masses directly over the wreckage. All throughout the night, the captain's normally carefree black Labrador whined and cowered, avoiding certain spots on the ship as if some invisible presence existed.

Bishop also noted that on October 21, 1975, a San Antonio psychic named J. Nickie Jackson recorded in her diary a dream she'd had that foretold the *Fitzgerald's* doom. In her dream, she saw the freighter struggling to stay afloat in giant waves before it finally plunged straight down into the depths. The real-life event occurred just three weeks later. Jackson was familiar with the *Edmund Fitzgerald* because she had previously lived in Superior but was surprised to dream about it in her new life in Texas.

The Loyal Keeper of the White River Light (Whitehall, Michigan)

Are you dedicated enough to your job to perform your duties until the day you die? What about the day after?

Western Michigan was filled with endless forests in the 1800s, providing a resource for building materials not only to Michigan but also to the fast growing cities of Chicago and Milwaukee nearby. The White River Light allowed vessels to safely pass from the lumber mills on the banks of White Lake, through the White River Channel, and into the shipping channels of Lake Michigan.

Let There Be Light

In the late 1850s, local mill owners and merchants became concerned about frequent shipwrecks occurring where the White River emptied into Lake Michigan near Whitehall, Michigan. The narrow river connected the lumber mills of White Lake (an area called "The Lumber Queen of the World") and the Great Lakes shipping channels. The state legislature responded by approving the construction of and funding for a lighthouse; however, the White River Light would not be built for another twelve years.

In 1872, a beacon light was set up at the area's South Pier, and shipping captain William Robinson was granted the position of light keeper. In 1875, the White River Light Station was built, and Robinson and his beloved wife, Sarah, moved into the keeper's residence, where they happily raised their eleven children. Robinson often said he was so happy there that he would stay until his dying day. That happiness was marred by Sarah's unexpected death in 1891. Robinson, who had expected to live with her at the lighthouse until his retirement, was inconsolable. Grief-stricken, he poured all of his attention into tending the lighthouse.

Like (Grand)father, Like (Grand)son

As Robinson grew older, the Lighthouse Board began to consider his replacement, finally awarding the post to his grandson (and assistant keeper), Captain William Bush, in 1915. Although the board expected Bush to immediately take over Robinson's duties, he kindly allowed his grandfather to continue as keeper and remain in the keeper's residence for several years.

In 1919, after forty-seven years of loyal service, the board demanded that Robinson vacate the premises, but he refused. The board allegedly met and agreed to take legal action against Robinson if he didn't leave, but they never got the chance. Two weeks later, on the day before the deadline, Robinson died in his sleep. Bush moved into the residence, and the board was satisfied with their new man. But Captain Robinson stayed on, apparently still refusing to budge.

Keeper Robinson was the oldest light keeper in service at the time of his death with forty-seven years of service at the age of eighty-seven.

Thump, Thump, Tap

The lighthouse was decommissioned in 1960 and was turned into a museum in 1970. Today, museum staff and visitors believe that Robinson still occupies the building and continues his duties as lighthouse keeper. Curator Karen McDonnell lives in the lighthouse and reports hearing footsteps on the circular staircase in the middle of the night. She attributes this to Robinson, rather than natural causes, because of the unmistakable sound of his walking cane on the stairs.

McDonnell believes Robinson may have also gotten his wish—to stay in the lighthouse with his wife—because Sarah seems to have returned to the lighthouse as well. She helps with dusting and light housework, leaving display cases cleaner than they were before. Museum visitors often talk about feeling warm and safe inside the building and feeling a sense of love and peace. One tourist felt the presence of a smitten young couple, sitting in one of the window nooks.

Today, visitors are welcome to explore the museum—open from June through October—and learn more about the shipping history of the Great Lakes.

Ghosts of Glensheen

In 1905, self-made millionaire Chester Congdon was one of Minnesota's richest men. When the banking and iron-mining magnate and his wife, Clara, moved into their stupendous mansion on the shore of Lake Superior in 1908, they never dreamed that their elegant home would someday be famous for murder and ghosts.

The Congdons named their sprawling estate "Glensheen." Chester Congdon only lived in his dream home for eight years: He died in 1916 at age sixty-three. The estate passed to Chester's widow, Clara, and then to the couple's youngest daughter, Elisabeth. To this day, the house retains most of the family's original furnishings, which makes this tragic residence even eerier to visitors.

The brick lakefront house features multiple gables and chimneys and thirty-nine richly furnished rooms. The Congdons spared no expense on their abode, equipping it with electricity, running water, and a humidification system and covering the grounds with lush gardens where they entertained Minnesota's elite with impressive parties.

Family Ties, Lies, and Sighs

In 1977, Elisabeth, Chester and Clara's youngest daughter, was eighty-three years old and was partially paralyzed. She had never married, although she had adopted two girls: Jennifer—who led a quiet life in Racine, Wisconsin—and Marjorie, the black sheep of the family. Elisabeth's life of luxury ended violently when an intruder smothered the helpless woman in her sleep with her own pink satin pillow; he also bludgeoned Elisabeth's protective night nurse, Velma Pietila, with a candlestick.

Suspicion immediately fell on Marjorie, but it was her husband, Roger Caldwell, who was charged with killing the elderly heiress to obtain Marjorie's $8 million share of the estate; Marjorie was charged with aiding and abetting him in the crime. Caldwell went to prison and later confessed to the crime, but Marjorie was acquitted. In fact, the trial's jurors felt so sorry for her that they threw her a posttrial party!

That was a nice gesture, but even being honored so highly was not enough to change Marjorie's basic nature. Although she did get her hands on a pile of her dead mother's money, her life deteriorated further thereafter. In 1981, she married Wallace Hagen (without divorcing Roger Caldwell), and in 1984, she was convicted of arson and insurance fraud in Minnesota. By 1992, Marjorie and Hagen were living in Arizona, where she was again found guilty of arson. After her conviction but before she went to jail, Hagen died of a mysterious drug overdose. Marjorie was arrested and charged with his murder, but the charges were later dropped.

Marjorie was released from prison in 2004, but in 2007, she was arrested again—this time on charges of committing fraud and forgery. In 2010, she again made headlines when she tried to get her probation dropped so that she could move into an assisted-living facility in Arizona.

The Glensheen estate was given as a gift to the University of Minnesota-Duluth in 1968. Elisabeth, in turn, was given a "life estate," allowing her to live on the estate until she died. The estate was opened as a museum two years after the murders occurred.

A Soft Sheen of Spirits

Meanwhile, Glensheen remains as grand as ever. Now owned by the University of Minnesota-Duluth, the mansion is used for art fairs and theatrical productions, including readings of the macabre stories of Edgar Allen Poe during Halloween season. The house and gardens are also open for public tours. And although its tour guides are reportedly tight-lipped about hauntings, it is believed that the spirits of Elisabeth and Velma have never left the place. People have seen misty figures floating about, heard unidentifiable noises, and felt cold chills when viewing the room in which Elisabeth died.

In one story that was recounted in *The Minnesota Road Guide to Haunted Locations*, an employee felt something pulling on his ankles while he was standing on a ladder. Thinking that a coworker had snuck up the ladder to play a prank, he turned to face the culprit, but no one was there—at least, no one that he could see.

Who could blame Elisabeth and Velma for lingering at the Glensheen Mansion? It's certainly a beautiful place to spend eternity.

Questions about the murder are not answered during the tour these days in order to respect the surviving members of the Congdon family. If tourists are looking for more information they can buy a book about the murders in the gift shop.

Five years before Elisabeth Congdon was killed, Patty Duke starred in a dark thriller filmed at Glensheen. The movie's title? *You'll Like My Mother*.

America's Haunted Lighthouses
(Various)

More than sixty lighthouses in the United States are believed to be haunted. Some are home to eerie ghosts, while others host more playful spirits. Whether they stick around because of tragedy, love, or some other reason, these spectral visitors add an otherworldly element to already-fascinating places.

St. Simons Island Lighthouse, Georgia

This lighthouse may have been cursed from the start. Originally constructed in 1811, the first building was destroyed by Confederate soldiers. While the lighthouse was being rebuilt, the architect fell ill and died of yellow fever. Then, on a stormy night in 1880, a dispute between the lighthouse keeper and his assistant resulted in gunshots. The keeper died after days of suffering from his wounds, but the assistant was never charged with the crime. The new keeper maintained he could hear strange footsteps on the spiral staircase to the tower. To this day, subsequent lighthouse keepers, their families, and visitors have also heard the same slow tread on the tower's 129 steps.

Boston Light, Massachusetts

The original Boston Light was the first lighthouse to be built by the American Colonies in 1716. In 1783, the original structure was replaced with a new lighthouse that still stands today as the second oldest lighthouse in the nation, next to Sandy Hook Lighthouse in New Jersey. The ghost that resides at the Boston Light is thought to be that of a sailor who was once guided by the beacon. Cold spots, phantom footsteps, empty rocking chairs that move back and forth on their own, and something eerie that makes cats hiss are all hallmarks of this haunted lighthouse. These are all typical behaviors for a ghost, but this one does have its quirks: Coast Guard members on the premises report that whenever they turn on a rock-and-roll radio station, the receiver suddenly switches to a classical music channel further down the dial.

Minots Ledge Lighthouse, Massachusetts

Despite the sweet nickname, the ghosts of the "I Love You" lighthouse tell a tragic story. The first Minots Ledge Lighthouse began operating in 1850, and being its keeper was arguably the most frightening assignment around. Built directly in the rough waters around the Cohasset Reefs, the spidery metal skeleton swayed and buckled in the wind and waves. On April 17, 1851, a sudden nor'easter stranded the keeper on the mainland—he could only watch as the storm slowly destroyed the lighthouse, with his two assistants inside. Their bodies were found after the storm cleared.

A new storm-proof stone tower was built, and the spirits of those who perished in the first lighthouse seem to reside in the new building. Subsequent keepers have heard them working, and sailors see them waving from the external ladder. On stormy nights the light blinks "one–four–three," which locals say is code for "I love you." They believe this is the assistants' message to their loved ones, passing ships, and anyone caught in a storm.

This is the second lighthouse that has occupied this site on Minots Ledge, a reef off of the harbor of Cohasset, Massachusetts. The first, built between 1847 and 1850, was washed away after only a few months of use during a storm that caused considerable amounts of damage to the Boston area. The new lighthouse was built between 1855 and 1860 and is supposedly "storm proof."

Yaquina Bay Lighthouse, Oregon

In 1899, Lischen M. Miller wrote a story for *Pacific Monthly* about a girl who disappeared at the Yaquina Bay Lighthouse. The girl, a captain's daughter, was left with a caretaker while her father was at sea. One day she and her friends went to explore the abandoned lighthouse. When she got separated from her friends, they heard her shriek. They searched for her but only found some blood and her handkerchief. A door that had been open only moments before was locked. Although many maintain that this story is pure fiction, the spectral figure of a girl has been seen around the tower.

St. Augustine Lighthouse, Florida

St. Augustine is often called America's most haunted city, and the lighthouse there might claim its own "most haunted" title. So many different spirits are rumored to haunt this light that it's probably a bit crowded. Visitors report seeing a young girl with a bow in her hair. She is thought to be the ghost of a girl who died during the tower's construction. A tall man is often seen in the basement of the keeper's house, and doors unlock mysteriously, footsteps follow visitors, and cold spots move around the buildings. The spirits seem harmless, but construction workers have complained of foreboding feelings and freak accidents.

A picture from 1824 of the original St. Augustine Light. This lighthouse was the first lighthouse built in Florida by the American government. The site was once the location of a Spanish watchtower built in the late 16th century.

Fairport Harbor Light, Ohio

This lighthouse is rumored to have two rather playful ghosts. The first is of a keeper's young son who died. The second appears to be a charming gray kitten that routinely seeks out museum staff and visitors to play. Its spectral nature becomes apparent when visitors realize the kitten has no feet—it simply hovers above the ground. Although a former keeper's wife had a beloved kitten while she lived in the lighthouse, the "ghost cat" story was dismissed as silly until workers found the body of a cat in a crawl space there.

Barnegat Lighthouse, New Jersey

If you travel with children, you may draw the attention of the ghosts at the Barnegat Lighthouse. According to legend, a couple was on a ship off the New Jersey coast when a severe storm struck. Feeling that the ship was safe, the man decided to stay aboard, and his wife stayed by his side. They did, however, send their baby ashore with one of the ship's mates. Although the ship survived the storm, the couple was not so lucky: They froze to death that winter night. Now, on cold, clear nights in January and February, their spirits approach other parents who are out for a stroll with their own infants. The friendly ghosts typically compliment the parents on their beautiful baby, and then they quickly disappear.

Old Presque Isle Lighthouse, Michigan

This lighthouse was decommissioned in 1870 and became a museum. In 1977, when George and Lorraine Parris were hired as caretakers, they ran the light regularly until the Coast Guard warned that running a decommissioned light was hazardous and illegal. To ensure it wouldn't happen again, the machinery that rotated the light was removed. But since George's death in 1992, the lighthouse has frequently glowed at night—not so brightly as to cause harm but bright enough to be seen by passing ships and across the bay. Although the Coast Guard has classified it as an "unidentified" light, Lorraine believes that it is George, still happily working in his lighthouse.

Phantom Ships and Ghostly Crews
(Various)

Ghost ships come in a variety of shapes and sizes, but they all seem to have the ability to slip back and forth between the watery veil of this world and the next, often making appearances that foretell of impending doom. Come with us now as we set sail in search of some of the most famous ghost ships in maritime history.

Princess Augusta

According to legend, shortly after Christmas 1738, the *Princess Augusta* ran aground and broke into pieces off the coast of Block Island, Rhode Island. Roughly 130 years later, poet John Greenleaf Whittier renamed the European vessel and told his version of the shipwreck in his poem "The Palatine," which was published in *Atlantic Monthly*. Today, strange lights, said to be the fiery ghost ship, are still reported in the waters surrounding Block Island, especially on the Saturday between Christmas and New Year's Day.

Mary Celeste

The *Amazon* was cursed from the beginning. During her maiden voyage, the *Amazon*'s captain died. After being salvaged by an American company that renamed her the *Mary Celeste*, the ship left New York on November 7, 1872, bound for Genoa, Italy. Onboard were Captain Benjamin Briggs, his family, and a crew of seven.

Nearly a month later, on December 4, the crew of the *Dei Gratia* found the abandoned ship. There was plenty of food and water onboard the *Mary Celeste*, but the only living soul on the ship was a cat. The crew and the captain's family were missing, and no clues remained as to where they went. The last entry in the captain's logbook was dated almost two weeks prior to the ship's discovery, meaning it had somehow piloted itself all that time.

To this day, the fate of the members of the *Mary Celeste* remains unknown, as does how the ship piloted its way across the ocean non-crewed for weeks. Many believe she was piloted by a ghostly crew that kept her safe until she was found.

Iron Mountain

A ship disappearing on the high seas is one thing, but on a river? That's exactly what happened to the *Iron Mountain*. In June 1872, the 180-foot-long ship left New Orleans heading for Pittsburgh via the Mississippi River with a crew of more than fifty men. A day after picking up additional cargo, which was towed behind the ship in barges, the *Iron Mountain* steamed its way north and promptly vanished. Later that day, the barges were recovered floating in the river, but the *Iron Mountain* and its entire crew were never seen nor heard from again. For years after it disappeared, ship captains would whisper to each other about how the *Iron Mountain* was simply sucked up into another dimension through a ghostly portal.

Flying Dutchman

Easily the world's most famous ghost ship, the story of the *Flying Dutchman* is legendary. Stories say that during the 1800s, a Dutch ship captained by Hendrick Vanderdecken was attempting to sail around the Cape of Good Hope when a violent storm came up. Rather than pull into port, the *Dutchman*'s stubborn captain claimed he would navigate around the Cape even if it took him all of eternity to do so. The ship and all of the crew were lost in the storm, and as foreshadowed by Vanderdecken, they were, indeed, condemned to sail the high seas for all eternity.

Almost immediately, people from all over the world began spotting the Dutch ship silently moving through the ocean, often cast in an eerie glow. Because of the legend associated with Captain Vanderdecken, sightings of the *Flying Dutchman* are now thought to be signs of bad things to come. Case in point: The most recent sighting of the vessel occurred off the coast of North Carolina's Outer Banks prior to Hurricane Isabel in 2003.

Lincoln Still Lingers in the White House (Washington, District of Columbia)

The Colonial-style mansion at 1600 Pennsylvania Avenue may be America's most famous residence, as well as one of the most haunted. Day and night, visitors and staff members have seen the spirits of past presidents, first ladies, and other former occupants. None of them are more celebrated than Abraham Lincoln, whose spirit is almost as powerful today as it was when he led America through the Civil War.

This photo taken by John Plumbe during the James K. Polk administration is the first known photograph of the White House.

Honest Abe Sees His Own Ghost

The morning after Abraham Lincoln was first elected president, he had a premonition about his death. He saw two reflections of himself in a mirror: One image showed how he usually appeared, fit and healthy; in the other, his face was pale and ghostly. Lincoln and his wife believed that the vision predicted that he wouldn't complete his second term in office.

Shortly before his assassination, Lincoln saw his own funeral in a dream. He said that he was in the White House, but it was strangely quiet and filled with mourners. Walking through the halls, he entered the East Room, where, to his horror, he saw a body wrapped in funeral vestments and surrounded by soldiers.

Lincoln said that in his dream, he approached one of the soldiers to find out what had happened. "Who is dead in the White House?" he demanded. "The president," the soldier replied. "He was killed by an assassin!"

A few days later—that fateful day when he attended Ford's Theatre for the last time—President Lincoln called a meeting of his cabinet members. He told them that they would have important news the following morning. He also explained that he'd had a strange dream…one that he'd had twice before. In it, he saw himself alone and adrift in a boat without oars. That was all he said, and the cabinet members left the president's office with a very uneasy feeling. The next day, they received the news that the president had been assassinated.

Two Wartime Leaders Meet

During World War II, the Queen's Bedroom was called the Rose Room. While visiting the White House, Winston Churchill strolled into the Rose Room completely naked and smoking a cigar after taking a bath. It was then that he encountered the ghost of Abraham Lincoln standing in front of the fireplace with one hand on the mantle, staring down at the hearth. Always a quick wit, Churchill said, "Good evening, Mr. President. You seem to have me at a disadvantage."

According to Churchill, Lincoln smiled at him and then vanished. Churchill refused to stay in the Rose Room again, but Lincoln wasn't finished surprising guests.

Hundreds of people have felt Lincoln's presence in the White House, and many have witnessed his apparition as well, including Eleanor Roosevelt's maid, who saw a spectral Abe sitting on a bed removing his boots.

President Lincoln has been seen in many places in the White House, but he appears most frequently in the Lincoln Bedroom. Although the late president's bed is now in this room, during his lifetime, the space served as the cabinet room in which he signed the Emancipation Proclamation.

Lincoln Disturbs the Queen

When Queen Wilhelmina of the Netherlands stayed in the Queen's Bedroom in 1945, she was hoping to get a good night's sleep. Instead, she was awakened by noisy footsteps in the corridor outside her room. Annoyed, she waited for whomever it was to return to his or her room, but the individual stopped at her door and knocked loudly several times. When the queen finally opened the door, she found herself face to face with the specter of Abraham Lincoln. She said that he looked a bit pale but very much alive and was dressed in travel clothes, including a stovepipe hat and coat. The queen gasped, and Lincoln vanished.

Lincoln's ghost may be the most solid-looking and "real" spirit at the White House, and hundreds of people have encountered it. Strangely enough, Lincoln seemed to be in touch with the Other Side even before he died: He once claimed that he saw his own apparition and talked about it often.

Aside from the vision of death Lincoln had in this room, there have been numerous funeral services conducted in the East Room throughout American history, including the funeral service for twelve-year-old Willie Lincoln, Abraham Lincoln's third son who died of typhoid fever in 1862.

Stephen Decatur's Former Home
(Washington, District of Columbia)

In Washington, D.C., a sullen figure stands at a window, looking at the world outside—even though he is a visitor from the Great Beyond. The figure is the ghost of Stephen Decatur, one of the country's greatest military heroes—long dead but condemned to prowl the halls of his former home.

Rising Star

In 1807, Stephen Decatur was already a war hero for the young United States. He garnered accolades for his bravery against the Barbary Pirates and for serving as a member of a naval commission that investigated the actions of Commodore James Barron. Barron was the commander of the U.S. frigate *Chesapeake*; after the British ship *Leopold* fired a shot across the *Chesapeake*'s bow, Barron boarded the *Leopold* and took four of its sailors into custody. At the time, tensions between Britain and America were running high, so the commission on which Decatur served was organized to investigate Barron's actions. It found that Barron had not received permission for his actions, so he was court-martialed and suspended for five years. Decatur spoke against Barron at the hearing, and Barron was not a man to forgive and forget.

When the War of 1812 broke out between the United States and England, Decatur took command of the *Chesapeake* and built up his reputation while Barron seethed on the sidelines. Then, in 1818, Decatur and his wife, Susan, became power players on the Washington, D.C., social scene after they built a house on fashionable Lafayette Square. However, Decatur's past would come back to haunt him. Over the years, Barron had unleashed a series of personal attacks on him. The whole affair culminated in early 1820 when Barron challenged Decatur to a duel.

One of the oldest surviving homes in the D.C. area, the Decatur House is one of the three still standing buildings in the U.S. designed by neoclassical architect Benjamin Henry Latrobe. Latrobe also designed the Washington Canal and worked as superintendent of construction for the U.S. Capitol.

Fallen Star

The night before the duel, Decatur stared glumly from his bedroom window, looking at his estate and the neighborhood. The next day, at a field in Maryland, Decatur—apparently channeling his inner Alexander Hamilton—attempted only to wound Barron (even though Decatur was an expert marksman). However, Barron—taking a page from Aaron Burr's playbook—shot to kill and mortally wounded his enemy. Decatur was carried home, where he died an agonizing death on March 22, 1820. While he lay dying, the heartbroken Susan could barely look at him because she was so upset.

While lying wounded in his home, it is reported that Decatur said, "I did not know that any man could suffer such pain."

Eternal Star

Soon after his death, people began seeing a figure staring sadly out of the window where Decatur himself had stood on the night before the duel. The ghost was seen so often that eventually the window was sealed up. But bricks and mortar can't keep a good ghost down—Decatur's apparition continued to manifest throughout the house and at other windows.

Today, the former Decatur home is a museum of White House history. However, that has not stopped the ghost of Stephen Decatur from roaming its halls and appearing in various rooms, always with an expression of infinite sadness on his face.

Sometimes, in the early morning hours, a figure is spotted leaving the building through the back door. It carries a black box—perhaps containing a dueling pistol—just as Decatur did on the last day of his life. Inside the house, people have felt unbelievable sadness and emptiness in the first-floor room where Decatur died.

However, Stephen Decatur is not the only restless spirit that haunts the Lafayette Square property. Disembodied sobbing and wailing have been heard throughout the house; some speculate that it's the ghost of Susan Decatur reliving her life's greatest sorrow.

The house is now a museum. The first floor has remained decorated in an untouched early 19th century design, while the second floor has been fit with more modern renovations. Because of the house's proximity to the White House and the fact that slaves worked in the house, the museum contains a considerable amount of information on African American history.

Westover Plantation
(Charles City County, Virginia)

She said that she wanted to return in a nice way, so as not to frighten anyone. And in the afterlife, Evelyn Byrd seems to have gotten her wish to become a friendly ghost.

The Westover Plantation began producing tobacco in 1665 and used the labor of hundreds of African American slaves who lived on the plantation grounds.

Love Byrd

Evelyn Byrd was born in 1707; her father was William Byrd II, who founded the city of Richmond, Virginia. When she was ten years old, Evelyn was sent to school in England. While she was away, she fell in love with someone whom her father disliked—as young girls sometimes do. And as fathers often do, William forced the lovebirds to end their relationship. A few years later, when a brokenhearted Evelyn returned to her father's Virginia estate—which was known as Westover Plantation—she simply withdrew from life. She only maintained contact with a friend named Anne Carter Harrison; the two girls met almost daily in a nearby poplar grove.

This continued for several years until one day, Evelyn confided to Anne that she felt the approach of death. However, she urged her friend to continue going to the poplar grove; she said that after her death, they would still meet there. Evelyn insisted that she would return but not in a scary sort of way.

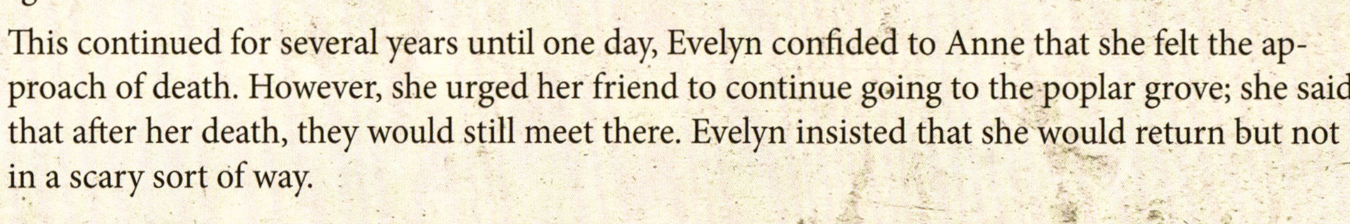

There have been numerous sightings of Evelyn Byrd's ghost walking under the trees in the front yard of the house.

The Genial Ghost

Evelyn's prophecy was correct: She died shortly thereafter at age twenty-nine. One day soon after, Anne was in the poplar grove when she saw Evelyn wearing a stunning white dress and strolling through the trees, just as she had in life. Evelyn smiled at Anne and then vanished. Thus began the sightings of Evelyn, both on the grounds of Westover and inside the house. What sets Evelyn apart from most ghosts is that she's often seen as a three-dimensional figure that's only identified as a ghost when she vanishes.

Once, when a workman walked into a bedroom at Westover to complete some repairs, he was startled to see a woman sitting in front of a mirror combing her hair. Surprised that the room was occupied, the workman told the homeowner about it. When they returned to the room, it was empty.

Clearly, Evelyn wants to be as unobtrusive as possible while still making her presence known. On another occasion, a girl visiting Westover awoke to see Evelyn—resplendent in her white dress—staring benignly at her. Another visitor woke up in the middle of the night, casually gazed out the window, and saw Evelyn standing on the front lawn. Evelyn motioned the woman away from the window, as if to say, "Go away. You've got all day. This is my time now." The guest obediently closed the drapes.

Sometimes, Evelyn just seems to want to be a part of the action at Westover, such as the time when she began following a person out of the house. Thinking that it was a friend, the person turned and gazed back to see a woman with black hair wearing a beautiful white dress. As soon as the two made eye contact, the woman in the white dress disappeared.

Byrds of a Feather Haunt Together

Evelyn does not hold a ghostly monopoly at Westover. Her sister-in-law, Elizabeth Hill Carter Byrd, had an unhappy marriage and died tragically in her bedroom when the heavy chest of drawers that she was searching for evidence of her husband's infidelity fell on top of her and crushed her. Even today, people hear horrible disembodied screams coming from her old bedroom; it is believed that Elizabeth is doomed to forever reenact her agonizing death.

Still another Westover ghost is that of Evelyn's brother, William Byrd III, who committed suicide in his bedroom in 1777 after he lost the family fortune due to his gambling. Once, a person who was spending the night in that room felt an icy cold presence enter and then watched it glide over to a chair. After that, the room was filled with an oppressive atmosphere, which the visitor suspected was caused by the spirit of William Byrd III.

But it's Evelyn, the friendly spirit, who holds the most sway at Westover, which proves that nice ghosts don't necessarily finish last.

William Byrd II's tomb can be found on the grounds of the plantation in the garden. His son, William Byrd III, eventually sold much of the land his father gave him to pay off gambling debts. Although William Byrd III raised huge amounts of money from the sales, he still could not pay his creditors and eventually committed suicide.

Ghosts of Harpers Ferry

(Harpers Ferry, West Virginia)

Harpers Ferry, West Virginia, is a picturesque town that has been at the center of a great deal of American history, most notably during the mid-19th century, when abolitionist John Brown staged a raid that proved to be a catalyst for the American Civil War. However, Harpers Ferry is also known for its ghosts.

Harpers Ferry was settled in 1747 when John Harper passed through the area. He recognized the potential for industry created by the powerful confluence of the Shenandoah and Potomac Rivers.

Rachael Harper

In the mid-18th century, Robert Harper founded the town of Harpers Ferry. After he and his wife Rachael lost their first house in a flood, Harper began construction of a much grander home. But this was during the American Revolution, when laborers were hard to find, so the aging Harper did much of the work himself. He was quite concerned about lawlessness during this uncertain time, so legend has it that he instructed Rachael to bury their gold in a secret location and tell no one about it. Harper passed away in 1782, and after Rachael died unexpectedly following a fall from a ladder, the secret location of their gold was buried with her.

For many years, the Harper House has been considered haunted. People who pass it swear that they see a woman in old-fashioned clothes staring out from an upstairs window. Perhaps it's Rachael, remaining watchful and vigilant over the family's gold.

This is the fourth house John Harper built in the area after the first three were devastated by continual flooding. Both he and his wife died before the building was completed. After their deaths, the building was used as a tavern. Historians claim that George Washington, Thomas Jefferson, and Meriwether Lewis all stayed at this house during their lifetimes.

St. Peter's Catholic Church

During the Civil War, St. Peter's Catholic Church was used as a hospital for wounded soldiers. One day, a wounded young soldier was brought into the churchyard and left lying on the ground as others with more severe injuries were tended to. Hours passed, and the young man's condition worsened as he slowly bled to death. By the time doctors got to him, it was too late. As he was carried into the church, he whispered weakly, "Thank God I'm saved." Then he died.

Over the years, many people have seen a bright light on the church's threshold and heard faint whispers say, "Thank God I'm saved." Some have also watched as an elderly priest emerges from the church's rectory; he turns and walks into the church—right through the wall where the front facade once stood.

St. Peter's Church was the only church in Harpers Ferry to escape the Civil War without being destroyed.

John Brown

John Brown is probably the most noteworthy figure associated with the town of Harpers Ferry. Many people are familiar with his tall, gaunt, white-bearded image, so perhaps it's not surprising that many have seen someone looking exactly like him wandering around town. The resemblance to Brown is so uncanny that tourists have taken photos with the spirit; however, when the pictures are developed, "Brown" is not in them.

John Brown's ghost has also been spotted several miles outside of town at the Kennedy Farmhouse. It was there that Brown and his men stayed for several months while planning the raid. Even today, phantom footsteps, disembodied male voices, and snoring can be heard coming from the empty attic where the conspirators once stayed. It's no wonder that particular area of the house is largely shunned.

Originally built to be used as a guard and fire-engine house, John Brown's Fort was captured by John Brown and his coconspirators of abolitionists and runaway slaves during their raid of Harpers Ferry. The raid ended with Brown and his crew of insurgents being captured by U.S. Marines. Brown was charged with killing four white men, treason against Virginia, and conspiring with slaves to rebel. He was hanged on December 2, 1859.

Spirits Live on at the West Virginia Penitentiary (Moundsville, West Virginia)

The fact that all of West Virginia's executions used to take place at the West Virginia Penitentiary is only one of the reasons why this prison has more than its fair share of ghosts. Torture, violence, murder, and suicide were all common occurrences during its 119 years in operation, so it's no wonder that some of the people who lived there still roam its dank, dark halls.

With the Gothic look of a spooky storybook castle, the West Virginia Penitentiary in Moundsville was built in the late 1800s. It was originally designed to house 480 inmates, but its population grew from 250 prisoners when it opened in 1876 to 2,400 in the early 1930s. With as many as three men sharing one tiny five-foot-by-seven-foot cell, living conditions there were atrocious.

The first phase of the West Virginia Penitentiary's construction began in 1867 and was finished in 1876. Prison labor was used to complete the main gate, the north and south cellblock areas, and the guard tower.

Beaten Spirits

Wardens at the West Virginia Penitentiary—which was once listed by the Department of Justice as one of the Top Ten Most Violent Correctional Facilities in the nation—issued severe punishments for those inmates who misbehaved: Prisoners were tortured, whipped, and beaten. One spirit that lingers there is believed to be that of Robert, an inmate who was beaten to death.

Over the years, many deaths occurred within the prison's walls. Some were brought on by violent treatment, poor living conditions, and illness; additionally, a total of ninety-four men were executed there: eighty-five by hanging and nine via the electric chair. One execution began with a mishap when a man who had been sentenced to hang fell through the floor before the noose could be fixed around his neck; he had to be picked up and taken back upstairs, where he was then hanged successfully. It is said that his spirit still wanders around the gallows where he died.

As early as the 1930s, folks at the prison began seeing ghosts and reporting an eerie feeling that an invisible entity was standing close by. One specter that is often seen is that of a tattletale maintenance man who spied on the inmates and liked to get them in trouble. He met his end when a group of prisoners attacked him in a bathroom, which is where his earthbound spirit remains today.

Ghostly activity has also been observed in the shower area, in the chapel, along death row, and at the execution site. And don't forget the front gate, where the turnstiles move by themselves—perhaps admitting a "new" batch of inmates.

One particularly frightening spirit at the West Virginia Pen is that of the "shadow man," whose misty shape has been spotted lurking in the dark, giving off a menacing feeling to those who see him. In fact, many of the spirits there are intimidating; they often leave people with a sense that they are being watched or even followed.

The West Virginia Penitentiary experienced a jailbreak in 1979 in which fifteen inmates escaped, leading to one inmate killing an off duty cop in Moundsville, eluding authorities, and gaining a spot on the FBI's Most Wanted List. Also, the prison endured a riot in 1986 where inmates overthrew six officers and held them hostage for two days.

Unruly Spirits

One area of the prison that investigators have found to be teeming with paranormal activity is known as "the Sugar Shack"—an area where inmates went to exercise. Although there is no official record of a death occurring there, many people have felt cold spots and heard unexplained noises, such as screams and arguing voices. Some visitors have even felt unseen hands poking them in the back or stroking them on the cheek.

If you like ghosts or history—or both—the West Virginia Pen is well worth the trip. But beware of this group of spirits: They were unhappy in life and are still unhappy in death. So if you feel the touch of something that you can't see, it might be a good idea to run.

The chapel was probably a place of refuge for many convicts who found themselves in this overcrowded prison. The prison was shut down in 1986 after the State of West Virginia found the confinement to five-by-seven-foot cells to be cruel and unusual punishment.

Cellblock 15, or Death Row, is known as a paranormal hotspot in the West Virginia Penitentiary. Ninety-four convicts passed through this hall to meet their fate by hanging until the electric chair was implemented in 1951. The public was allowed to view hangings up until June 19, 1931, when convict Frank Hyer was decapitated after his weight settled into the noose.

The Ghosts of Antietam
(Sharpsburg, Maryland)

With nearly 23,000 total casualties, the Battle of Antietam was one of the bloodiest single-day skirmishes of the American Civil War. More than 3,600 of these men died suddenly and violently that day—ripped out of this world and sent reeling into the next. It's no wonder that the ghosts of some of these soldiers still haunt the Antietam battlefield in western Maryland. Perhaps they're still trying to understand what happened to them on that terrible day.

Gaelic Ghosts

Bloody Lane at Antietam National Battlefield is a sunken road that's so named because of the incredible slaughter that took place there on September 17, 1862. One of the notable battalions that fought at Bloody Lane was the Union's Irish Brigade, which lost more than sixty percent of its soldiers that day. The brigade's Gaelic war cry was *faugh-a-ballaugh* (pronounced fah-ah-bah-LAH), which means "clear the way."

Many years ago, a group of schoolchildren took a class trip to Antietam. After touring the battlefield, several boys walked down Bloody Lane toward an observation tower that had been built where the Irish Brigade had charged into the battle. Later, back at the school, the boys wrote that they heard odd noises coming from a nearby field. Some said that it sounded like a chant; others, however, likened the sounds to the "fa-la-la-la-la" portion of the Christmas carol "Deck the Halls." Did the boys hear the ghostly battle cry of the Irish Brigade?

On another occasion, some battle reenactors were lying on the ground near the Bloody Lane when they suddenly began hearing a noise that they were very familiar with—the sound of a regiment marching in full battle gear. Their experience as reenactors allowed them to pick out specific sounds, such as knapsacks, canteens, and cartridge boxes rattling and scraping. However, no matter how hard they looked, the men could see no marching soldiers. They concluded that the sounds were made by an otherworldly regiment.

Prying Eyes

Because of its strategic location on the battlefield, the Phillip Pry House was pressed into service as a makeshift hospital during the battle. Much misery took place there, including the death of Union General Israel B. Richardson, despite the loving care of his wife Frances. In 1976, the house was damaged by fire, and one day during the restoration, the wife of a park ranger met a woman dressed in Civil War-era attire coming down the stairs. She asked her husband who the woman was, but he had no knowledge of a woman in period clothes at the park.

Later, a woman was seen staring out an upstairs window in the room where General Richardson died. Nothing was particularly unusual about this…except that the room was being renovated at the time and didn't have a floor. Was it the ghost of Frances Richardson, still trying to take care of her dying husband? Members of the construction crew that was working at the house decided that this was not the project for them and abandoned it immediately after sighting this female phantom. Disembodied footsteps have also been reported going up and down the home's stairs.

A Bridge Between Two Worlds

Burnside Bridge was another scene of massive slaughter at Antietam, as Union troops repeatedly tried to take the tiny stone span only to be driven back by intense Confederate fire. Many of the soldiers who died there were quickly buried in unmarked graves near the bridge, and now it seems as if that arrangement wasn't to their liking. Many credible witnesses, including park rangers, have reported seeing blue balls of light floating near the bridge at night. The faint sound of a phantom drumbeat has also been heard in the vicinity.

Although the Battle of Antietam took place around 150 years ago, it seems that in some places, the battle rages on—and for some, it always will.

America's Most Haunted Lighthouse
(St. Mary's County, Maryland)

Built in 1830, the historic Point Lookout Lighthouse is located in St. Mary's County, Maryland, where the Potomac River meets Chesapeake Bay. It is a beautiful setting for hiking, boating, fishing, camping, and ghost-hunting.

Point Lookout was the place of a Confederate soldier prison. The soldiers who ended up there were subjected to limited food rations and severe weather.

Nighttime tours of the lighthouse are available to help raise funds to preserve the site from vandals and other trespassers.

The Most Ghosts

Point Lookout Lighthouse has been called America's most haunted lighthouse, perhaps because it was built on what later became the largest camp for Confederate prisoners of war.

Marshy surroundings, tent housing, and close quarters were a dangerous combination, and smallpox, scurvy, and dysentery ran rampant. The camp held more than 50,000 soldiers, and between 3,000 and 8,000 died there.

Park rangers and visitors to the lighthouse report hearing snoring and footsteps, having a sense of being watched, and feeling the floors shake and the air move as crowds of invisible beings pass by. A photograph of a former caretaker shows the misty figure of a young soldier leaning against the wall behind her, although no one noticed him when the photo was taken during a séance at the lighthouse. And a bedroom reportedly smelled like rotting flesh at night until the odor was publicly attributed to the spirits of the war prisoners.

The Lost Ghost

In December 1977, Ranger Gerald Sword was sitting in the lighthouse's kitchen on a stormy night when a man's face appeared at the back door. The man was young, with a floppy cap and a long coat, and peered into the bright room. Given the awful weather, Sword opened the door to let him in, but the young man floated backward until he vanished entirely. Later, after a bit of research, Sword realized he had been face-to-face with Joseph Haney, a young officer whose body had washed ashore after the steamboat he was on sank during a similar storm in 1878.

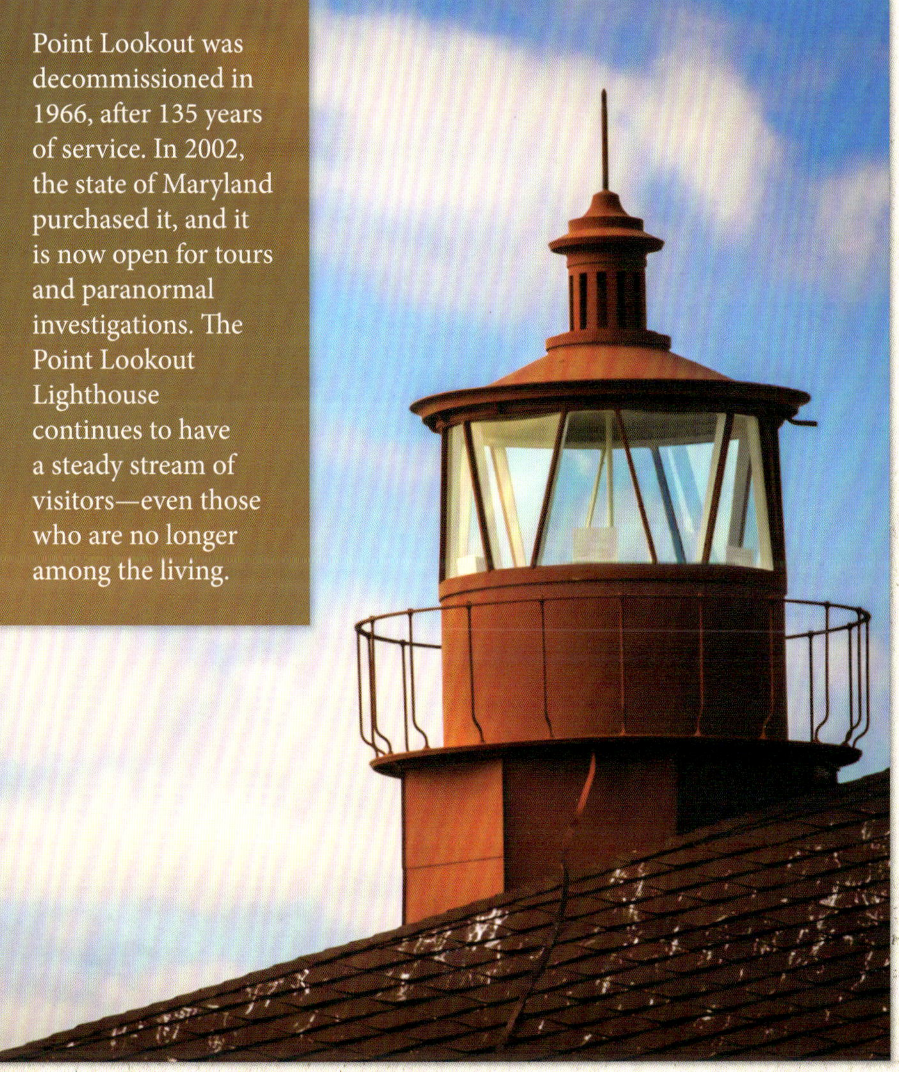

Point Lookout was decommissioned in 1966, after 135 years of service. In 2002, the state of Maryland purchased it, and it is now open for tours and paranormal investigations. The Point Lookout Lighthouse continues to have a steady stream of visitors—even those who are no longer among the living.

The Host Ghost

One of Point Lookout's most frequent visitors is the apparition of a woman dressed in a long blue skirt and a white blouse who appears at the top of the stairs. She is believed to be Ann Davis, the wife of the first lighthouse keeper. Although her husband died shortly after he took the post, Ann remained as the keeper for the next thirty years, and, according to inspection reports, was known for clean and well-kept grounds. Caretakers claim to hear her sighing.

Who Said That?

Point Lookout's reputation drew Hans Holzer, Ph.D., a renowned parapsychologist, who tried to capture evidence of ghostly activity. Holzer and his team claimed to have recorded twenty-four different voices in all, both male and female, talking, laughing, and singing. Among their recordings, the group heard male voices saying "fire if they get too close," "going home," and more than a few obscenities.

Take Care, Caretaker

One former caretaker reported waking in the middle of the night to see a ring of lights dancing above her head. She smelled smoke and raced downstairs to find a space heater on fire. She believes that the lights were trying to protect her and the lighthouse from being consumed by flames.

St. Louis Cemetery Is Number One Among Spirits (New Orleans, Louisiana)

In one of the most haunted cities in America, you're bound to find ghosts if you know where to look. And even if you don't, keep in mind that old buildings, new buildings, and cemeteries all attract restless spirits. Among the cemeteries in New Orleans, one is known as the most haunted of them all—St. Louis Cemetery No. 1.

St Louis Cemetery No. 1 was built to replace the older St. Peter Cemetery as the city's burial ground after the fire of 1788.

Looking Spooky

When European immigrants first settled in New Orleans, they needed a place to bury their dead. Unfortunately in New Orleans, that isn't as easy as it sounds. The city lies below sea level, so anything buried (i.e., a coffin) eventually pops back up to the surface due to the water level. That's why the city is full of above ground cemeteries where the dead are encased in tombs or vaults. So instead of the tiny tombstones you see in graveyards in other parts of the country, the cemeteries in New Orleans are full of structures that are large enough to hold a coffin (or several). Those cemeteries are known as "cities of the dead."

Near the French Quarter, you'll find St. Louis Cemetery No. 1. Established in 1789, it's a beautiful place that's full of historical significance…and ghosts. In fact, many consider it the most haunted cemetery in the United States.

Just the look of St. Louis Cemetery No. 1 is enough to send a shiver down your spine. That's probably why it has been featured in several Hollywood movies, including *Easy Rider* (1969) and *Interview with the Vampire* (1994).

New Orleans is known for its eclectic mix of cultures, and the variety of burial traditions on display at St. Louis Cemetery No. 1 showcase this. French, Irish, and Spanish settlers are among the earliest people who were buried there, and today, their marble tombs mix with crumbling rocks. The graveyard's narrow rows and winding paths lead to dead ends and confusion.

The cemetery contains thousands of buried people within a one block radius, with most of the gravesites being above-ground vaults built in the 18th and 19th centuries.

It's no wonder that visitors report hearing eerie sounds surrounding them in this otherworldly place. Is it the wind? Or is it the sound of spirits filling the air with their weeping and moaning?

Ghostly figures and phantom mists hover near the tombs. Some of the spirits are thought to be well-known people; others are anonymous but no less frightening.

Various figures from New Orleans' past are buried here, including Bernard de Marigny (a French-Creole aristocrat), Barthelemy Lafon (one of Jean Lafitte's pirates), Paul Morphy (an early world chess champion), and Benjamin Latrobe (the second architect of the U.S. Capitol). Nicolas Cage has also purchased a pyrimad-shaped tomb in the cemetery to be his final resting place.

Downcast Spirits

One oft-seen spirit is "Henry," who gave the deed to his tomb to a lady friend to have on hand when he died. Unbeknownst to him, she sold the plot while he was still alive, and upon his death some years later, he was buried in a potter's field. To this day, Henry is seen wandering through the cemetery, perhaps searching for a better place to spend his eternal rest. Some say that he has even asked mourners if there would be room for him in their loved one's tomb.

And if you like animals, St. Louis Cemetery No. 1 is a place to meet a few pets that are quite low maintenance. Ghosts of dogs and cats wander along the rows. All are friendly and are thought to be pets that belonged to a 19th-century groundskeeper. They seem to be looking for their beloved master.

Voodoo Resides Here

The most famous spirit at St. Louis Cemetery No. 1, however, is that of Marie Laveau. Considered the Voodoo Priestess of New Orleans, Laveau died in 1881, but her spirit still haunts these grounds. Some say that she comes alive each year on June 23 (St. John's Eve) to lead her Voodoo followers. Between these periods of resurrection, her spirit is often seen wearing a distinctive red-and-white turban with seven knots. And if you don't happen to spot her ghost, you might just hear her mumbling Voodoo curses. She has also been known to appear in feline form as a huge black cat; you'll recognize this specter by its glowing red eyes.

Those brave enough to approach Laveau's tomb will want to heed this ritual: Make three *X*s on the tombstone, turn around three times, and then knock three times on the stone, and your wish will be granted. And whatever you do, be sure to leave an offering—you definitely don't want to anger the Voodoo priestess.

Marie Laveau is believed to be buried in the plot 347 of St. Louis Cemetery No. 1, the Glapion family crypt. There are rumors that The Misfits, a New Jersey punk band, were once arrested for trying to disinter Laveau's body after they played a local concert.

There are three St. Louis cemeteries throughout the city of New Orleans. St. Louis Cemetery No. 1 is the oldest while the second and third date from 1823 and 1854.

No Ghostly Groupie for This Celeb

Apparently, celebrities don't intimidate ghosts. Actor Charles S. Dutton has been in more than eighty films and TV shows—including *Rudy* (1993), *Roc*, and *The L Word*—but that didn't matter to one ghostly resident of St. Louis Cemetery No. 1. As Dutton recounted in an episode of *Celebrity Ghost Stories*, he was in New Orleans directing a movie in 2006, when he and his girlfriend decided to visit the old cemetery to look for the grave of Marie Laveau.

After much searching, they found the tomb and were admiring the many offerings in front of it when they noticed that a nearby grave—which was marked "Duplessy 1850"—had been broken open. The casket was pulled out and its lid was open about five inches. Pure curiosity made them look inside, where they saw a skeleton with a colorful scarf around its neck. Dutton decided to close the coffin and shove it back into the tomb so that it wasn't exposed to the elements. It was getting late by then and his girlfriend pleaded with him to leave, but he kept working.

Suddenly, the couple felt a presence behind them. They turned and saw a raggedly dressed man wearing the same scarf around his neck as the skeleton in the coffin. The two men made eye contact, and Dutton described the moment as feeling as though the man was looking straight through his soul. The man eventually turned around and walked away, but when Dutton tried to follow him, he simply turned a corner and vanished. Dutton was convinced that he and his girlfriend had just met Mr. Duplessy, the man into whose casket they had just peered.

Beginning in March 2015, the cemetery was closed to the public by the Roman Catholic Diocese of New Orleans, who owns and operates the cemetery, because of the rise of vandalism occurring on the property.

Ghosts Gather at the Carter House (Franklin, Tennessee)

Before the Blood

In 1830, Fountain Branch Carter built a beautiful home in the heart of Franklin. In 1858, Johann Lotz constructed his own house across the street on land that he'd purchased from Carter. Both were blissfully unaware of what would occur there just a few years later.

After the fall of Nashville in 1862, Franklin became a Union military post. In 1864, in an attempt to "take the bull by the horns," the Confederate army decided to attack the enemy head-on in Franklin, hoping to drive General Sherman's army north. It didn't quite work out that way; instead, during the Battle of Franklin on November 30, 1864, more than 4,000 lives were lost, and because the battlefield was small, the concentration of bloodshed was very high. And most of it took place right in front of the Lotz and Carter homes.

In 1953, the Carter House was opened to the public. Today, it's a museum and a National Historic Landmark; its eight acres stand as a tribute to the battle that took place there so long ago. If you look closely, more than a thousand bullet holes can be found on the property.

The Battle Begins

When the Confederate troops arrived in town, Union General Jacob Cox commandeered the Carter House as his base of operations. Fearing for their lives, the Carter family took refuge in the basement during the five long hours of the battle. In all, twenty-three people—including the Lotz family—crowded into the cellar. They all survived, and when the fighting was over, both houses were converted into field hospitals. Surgeries, amputations, and death filled the days and weeks that followed. Between the violence and the chaos, it's no wonder that some of the dead never found peace.

The Lotz House—which was added to the National Historic Register in 1976 and opened to the public in 2008—bears its share of scars as well. Bloodstains are evident throughout, and a round indentation in the wood floor is a reminder of a cannonball that crashed through the roof, flew through a second-floor bedroom, and landed in the parlor on the first floor, leaving a charred path in its wake.

One of the men killed during the battle was Tod Carter, Fountain's son and a Confederate soldier who was thrilled to be heading home. He was wounded just 300 feet from his front door and was taken to his sister's bedroom, where he later died. Some say that his spirit remains there today.

In the Spirit of Things

Visitors to the Carter House have reported seeing the specter of Tod Carter sitting on a bed or standing in the hallway. His sister Annie has also been spotted in the hallways and on the stairs. She's blamed for playful pranks such as rolling a ball along the floor and causing objects to appear and disappear. But then again, the mischief-maker might be the spirit of one of the children who took refuge in the cellar during the battle. After all, staff members and visitors have reported feeling the sensation of a child tugging at their sleeves, and one worker even saw a spectral child walking down the staircase.

The ghosts of soldiers and other family members may be responsible for some of the other unusual phenomena experienced in the house, such as furniture moving on its own, doors slamming, and apparitions peering through the windows.

Not to be outdone, the ghosts at the Lotz House manifest as phantom voices and household items that move on their own or come up missing. While they haven't been identified, they seem to be civilian spirits rather than military ones. It's tough sharing space with so many ghosts, but the staff members are used to it, and they're happy to share the history—and the spirits—with visitors who stop by on the Franklin on Foot Ghost Tour. And don't worry: These lively spirits have never followed anyone home—at least not yet!

Ghosts of Shiloh

(Hardin County, Tennessee)

The Battle of Shiloh was a major conflict in the American Civil War. After the smoke cleared, tales of resurrected soldiers flowed almost as freely as the blood that precipitated their rise.

The Battle of Shiloh was a conflict in the Western Theater of the Civil War in which the Union Army of Tennesee, under Major General Ulysses S. Grant, who were camped along the Tennessee River at Pittsburg Landing, were surprise attacked by General Albert Sisney Johnston's Confederate Army of Mississippi.

Taking place on April 6 and 7, 1862, in southwestern Tennessee, the Battle of Shiloh proved sobering. It resulted in more than 23,000 casualties and made Union and Confederate soldiers realize that they were in for a protracted, bloody war. After the battle, tales of ghostly uprisings became commonplace. One of the most frequently told stories centered on the "Bloody Pond," where the injured cleaned their wounds during the battle, their blood staining the water a crimson shade. Since then, eyewitness accounts have claimed that every so often, the haunted pond turns blood red. Other reports told of ghostly shadow figures dressed as soldiers that continued to fight the battle, usually after sundown.

After the battle, slave owners and southern protectionists grew increasingly worried that their way of life was coming to an end, and when the Civil War came to a close in 1865, their fears were realized as hundreds of thousands of newly released slaves roamed the countryside in the South. However, six white supremacists in Pulaski, Tennessee (which is approximately ninety miles east of the battle site), stumbled upon a tactic that they hoped would help frighten the newly freed slaves back into passivity.

During a night of raucous behavior, the bumbling group dressed in sheets and rode drunk through the streets of Pulaski. They soon learned that frightened former slaves who had seen them that night believed them to be the legendary spirits of Shiloh. Realizing the possibilities, the group—which called itself the KyKlos Klan—posed as "ghosts" and staged countless raids during the Reconstruction period. Eventually, their fledgling organization would come to be known by a more familiar name: the Ku Klux Klan. Real or imagined, the Confederate ghosts of Shiloh had made their presence felt.

Sounds of gunfire, screams, and Rebel yells are said to accompany the otherworldly skirmishes that continue to happen around Bloody Pond after sundown.

The Sunken Road, or Hornet's Nest, was a major defensive line for the Union soldiers during the battle. Rather than bypassing the position, the Confederates assaulted the line several times over a number of hours, leading to a large number of Confederate casualties. It took nearly eight to fourteen separate charges on the position to force Union troops to surrender their position.

Dead Men Tell Tales
(Outer Banks, North Carolina)

In recent years, American moviegoers have gone gaga over pirates. Perhaps the most famous buccaneer of all was Edward Teach, better known as Blackbeard. His career was built on fear and intimidation, and apparently he hasn't changed—even in death.

The Devil of the Deep Blue Sea

Blackbeard's reign of terror on the high seas lasted for more than two years. During that time, he commanded a fleet of captured vessels and ambushed any ship he pleased. He pillaged and murdered up and down the East Coast until he turned himself in and was pardoned in July 1718.

After receiving his pardon, it didn't take long for Blackbeard to return to a life of piracy. In November 1718, Virginia Governor Alexander Spotswood ordered Lieutenant Robert Maynard to capture Blackbeard. On November 22, Maynard and his men finally caught up with the famed pirate and his crew just off Ocracoke Island. A battle ensued, during which Blackbeard and Maynard exchanged gunfire. The men then drew their swords, and Blackbeard managed to break Maynard's blade, but before he could kill the officer, a member of Maynard's party slit Blackbeard's throat. It took a total of five gunshot wounds and twenty sword strokes to bring down the notorious pirate, and to ensure that he was dead, he was decapitated; his head was suspended from the bowsprit of Maynard's vessel.

Edward Teach was born in Bristol, England, in 1680 and died in North Carolina in 1718. In his thirty-eight years, he caused havoc in the West Indies and the Atlantic coastal states of America. In his notorious career, he successfully blockaded the port of Charleston, South Carolina and ransomed its inhabitants, overtook multiples ships, and received a royal pardon for his crimes.

It is believed that Teach's parents moved to Jamaica when Teach was a young boy. Teach may have been a privateer in the Queen Anne's War before he moved to New Providence in the Bahamas, a home base for pirates in the 18th century, and joined the pirate crew of Captain Benjamin Hornigold.

Home Is Where the Head Is

Since that fateful day, Blackbeard's bloody specter has been seen on Ocracoke Island carrying a lantern, apparently searching for his missing head. The island is known locally as "Teach's Hole," and visitors and residents alike have reported seeing his phantom swimming along the shore at night; some have even watched him rise up from his watery grave and continue his search along the shore. Fishermen in Pamlico Sound have dubbed any strange lights viewed on North Carolina's Outer Banks "Teach's Lights." The few souls brave enough to follow the unearthly glow of Blackbeard's lantern ashore never find footprints or other signs of life when they investigate. Try as he might to find his missing head, some local legends suggest that Blackbeard is looking for his noggin in the wrong place.

Death to Spotswood!

In the 1930s, North Carolina judge Charles Whedbee claimed to have seen Blackbeard's skull. According to the judge, when he was in law school at the University of North Carolina, he was invited to join a secret society. His induction into the group involved a large silver chalice and the chanting of the mysterious phrase, "Death to Spotswood." Whedbee was told that a silversmith had made the cup from Blackbeard's skull after stealing it from atop a pole at the mouth of the Hampton River more than two centuries prior. The macabre chalice seems to have been lost to time, but it isn't the only treasure that Blackbeard is said to have left behind.

Blackbeard's Lady

Another legend suggests that Blackbeard left two treasures on Lunging Island—which is located off the coast of New Hampshire—during his reign of terror. One was a large amount of silver; the other was his wife, Mary Ormond. Over the years, several expeditions have undertaken quests to find the missing treasure, but always to no avail. However, many people have encountered the wispy figure of a woman wandering along the beach at night. Legend has it that she was Blackbeard's wife and that she was left behind to guard his loot.

There are varying accounts of how many casualties resulted from Maynard's attack on Blackbeard's crew. Maynard reports that he lost eight men while twelve pirates were killed, including Blackbeard himself. Blackbeard's body was dumped into the Ocracoke Inlet while his head was kept as proof to collect the reward promised by Spotswood.

Capitol Ghosts
(Raleigh, North Carolina)

Ghosts abound in North Carolina, but Raleigh—the state's capital since 1792—seems to be home to more than its share of playful poltergeists. The ghost of former governor Daniel Fowle haunts the North Carolina Executive Mansion, which has been the official residence of the state's governor since 1891. But whereas the governor's mansion holds just one ghost, the State Capitol is practically overflowing with spooks, almost all of whom prefer to make their presence known late at night.

The North Carolina State Capitol was completed in 1840. Its cornerstone was laid with Masonic honors by the Grand Master of North Carolina Masons on July 4th, 1833.

Weird Sounds

Longtime security guard Owen Jackson reported numerous encounters with the ghosts of the Capitol building. On several occasions, he heard the sound of books falling in the authentically restored state library on the third floor. But when he investigated the noises, no books were missing from the shelves or found on the floor.

Once in 1981, Jackson heard the sound of glass breaking on an upper floor; he fetched a broom to clean it up, but he found all of the windows intact and nothing else was broken. And on several occasions, Jackson heard mysterious footsteps and the sound of the building's elevator moving from floor to floor, as if transporting unseen visitors.

Another time, Jackson was sitting at the receptionist's desk preparing to make his rounds when he felt a hand rest on his shoulder. He quickly whirled around, but no one was there.

The building has not received major renovations since 1840.

Watchful Wraiths

Jackson isn't the only person who has encountered the Capitol's ghosts. Late one evening, curator Raymond Beck felt the eerie sensation that someone was looking over his shoulder as he shelved some books in the building's library. After it happened a second time, Beck didn't wait around for it to happen again—he finished his chore and left as quickly as possible.

Later, Beck told Sam Townsend Sr., an administrator at the Capitol building, about his bizarre experiences. Townsend admitted that he, too, had heard and felt things there that he couldn't explain. One evening in 1976, for example, Townsend was finishing up some paperwork when he heard a key rattling in the lock of the Capitol's north entrance. He assumed that it was Secretary of State Thad Eure returning to his office to catch up on some work (as was his habit), but when Townsend went to say hello, Eure was nowhere to be found. As Townsend stood near the north entrance, he suddenly heard keys rattling at the south entrance. He searched the building from top to bottom but found no logical explanation for the mysterious noises.

On another occasion, Townsend was again working late when he heard footsteps approaching from elsewhere on the same floor. Thinking that it was Beck, Townsend went to Beck's office to let him know that he was there too, but the room was empty. Townsend heard the same phantom footsteps on several occasions and always at the same time—8:30 p.m.

Seen and Heard

Townsend is one of the few people to see the Capitol ghosts as well as hear them. Once, Townsend walked by the Senate chamber on his way to his office and was startled to see someone standing just inside the chamber's doorway. But when he checked to make sure that his eyes weren't deceiving him, the figure had vanished.

The North Carolina State Capitol was declared a National Historic Landmark in 1973.

Another time, Townsend almost bumped into a ghost that floated by him in the rotunda. Recalling the incident, Townsend said that he stepped aside quickly so as to "avoid a collision."

Owen Jackson also caught a glimpse of one of the spirits that dwells within the Capitol building. One night after he finished his rounds, he turned off all but the security lights, checked all the doors, and then exited the building and walked to his car. As he waited for his vehicle to warm up, Jackson glanced up and saw a man walk past an illuminated window on the second floor. According to Jackson, the figure was wearing the uniform of a Confederate soldier.

Rather than investigate, Jackson simply went home. As he later told a reporter, "I figured anybody [that's] been dead that long, I didn't want to tangle with him."

Fort Delaware Prison Hosts Ghosts Through the Ages (Delaware City, Delaware)

Pea Patch Island. Sounds quaint, doesn't it? Hardly the name of a place that you'd imagine would host a military prison...or the ghosts of former inmates who still can't seem to escape, even in death. But then, the hardships and horrors that were experienced there might just trump the loveliness that the name suggests.

With no extra blankets or clothing, Fort Delaware's inmates struggled to keep warm and suffered through the cold, harsh winters that are typical in the mid-Atlantic region. Malaria, smallpox, and yellow fever were commonplace, and they traveled quickly through the facility; estimates suggest that between 2,500 and 3,000 people may have died there—and many tormented souls seem to remain.

Shaped like a pentagon, Fort Delaware Prison was completed in 1859, just prior to the Civil War. With a moat surrounding its thirty-two-foot-high walls, it was a very secure place to hold Confederate POWs.

The first Confederate soldier to have died within the confines of the fort was Captian L. P. Halloway on April 9, 1862. Halloway's body was identified and reclaimed by his family after the war had ended.

Now Appearing . . .

One ghost that has been seen by many workers at the Fort Delaware Prison—which is now a living-history museum—is not the spirit of a prisoner at all: It's that of a former cook who now spends her time hiding ingredients from the current staff. Visitors have reported hearing a harmonica in the laundry area, where a ghost has been spotted threading buttons in a long string. In the officer's quarters, a spectral child is known to tug on people's clothes and a ghostly woman taps visitors on the shoulder. Books fall from shelves, and chandelier crystals swing back and forth by themselves. And then there are the darker, more sinister spirits—the ones that suffered in life and found no relief in death. Moans, muffled voices, and rattling chains fill the basement with spooky sounds of prisoners past.

Ghost Hunter Endorsed

If you're searching for proof that these ghosts are the real deal, check out a 2008 episode of *Ghost Hunters* that was shot at Fort Delaware. Jason Hawes, Grant Wilson, and their team of investigators found quite a bit of paranormal activity when they visited the old prison. In the basement's tunnels, they heard unexplained footsteps and voices, as well as something crashing to the ground. A thermal-imaging camera picked up the apparition of a man who appeared to be running away from the group. And in the kitchen, the investigators heard a very loud banging sound that seemingly came from nowhere.

There were 11,000 Confederate prisoners in the fort by August 1863, and that number went up to 33,000 by the end of the war.

In the Spirit of Things

It's not *all* terror at the old prison. Today, Fort Delaware is part of a state park that's open to tourists and offers many special programs. One event that appeals to athletes and history buffs alike is the "Escape from Fort Delaware" triathlon: Each year when the starting musket blasts, participants reenact the escape route of fifty-two inmates who broke out of Fort Delaware Prison during the Civil War.

The parade grounds and Officer's Quarters are pictured here. Nearly half of all the deaths that occurred within the fort were from a smallpox epidemic. Some 200 prisoners died of typhoid or malaria, 70 from scurvy, and 61 from pneumonia. Some 109 Union soldiers and 40 civilians died there as well.

The Spirit Who Likes Spirits

(Dover, Delaware)

Located in Dover, Delaware, Woodburn was constructed in the late 1700s and is a classic example of Colonial-style architecture. Before it became the official governor's mansion in 1965, it had several owners, as well as several ghosts—including one with a fondness for alcohol spirits.

According to legend, early owners of the house frequently left wine-filled decanters out for the thirsty entity, only to find them completely empty the next morning. One staff member claimed to have actually seen the ghost enjoying its beverage; he described the specter as an older man who was wearing Colonial-era attire, including a powdered wig. Former owner Dr. Frank Hall told friends that he occasionally found mysteriously empty wine bottles in the pantry.

The property Woodburn was built upon was granted to David Morgan in 1684 by the Swedish crown. Charles Hillyard III bought the land at a sheriff's sale for $110 in the 1780s. It was Hillyard who built the Woodburn house in 1790.

A Host of Ghosts

The spirit-loving spirit may be the most active ghost in the house, but it isn't the only one that resides there. In 1805, an apparition nicknamed "the Colonel" made an appearance before evangelist Lorenzo Dow, who was in town for a series of revival meetings. Dow mentioned to his hosts that he had passed a gentleman in the upstairs hall; the hosts were surprised because Dow was their only guest at the time.

Other ghosts that have been witnessed at Woodburn include a young girl wearing a checkered gingham dress and a man who, in life, was rumored to have been involved in slave kidnapping and is known for rattling chains on the grounds of the estate.

The slave kidnapper was part of a pro-slavery mob that attacked the mansion, which was a stop on the Underground Railroad at the time; however, the mob was rebuked by a group of Quakers. According to legend, the kidnapper hid in an old tree, where he hanged himself. Whether his death was an accident or a suicide remains a mystery; either way, the incident seems to have kept his spirit earthbound.

The Woodburn property has passed through many owners since it was built. It was home to a school from 1953 to 1965.

Flagler College:
Hosting Ghosts in Style (St. Augustine, Florida)

Tycoon Henry Morrison Flagler certainly makes his presence known at his former luxury hotel, which is now home to Ponce de León Hall on the campus of Flagler College. The building houses the school's administrative offices and a women's dormitory. Flagler's second wife, his mistress, and several other earthbound spirits also join him there.

An eccentric businessman, Flagler retired to Florida in the late 1800s and built his hotel. Fascinated with death, he instructed hotel staffers that when he died, the doors and windows were to be left open so that his spirit could easily cross over. However, when Flagler passed away in 1913, a janitor unknowingly shut every door and window, and it is said that in its haste to leave, Flagler's spirit bounced off a closed window and landed on a floor tile, where his face is allegedly still seen to this day. He also reportedly plays pranks on students at the college that bears his name.

The Ponce de León Hall, once the Ponce de León Hotel, was built by Standard Oil cofounder Henry M. Flagler in 1888.

The Ponce de León Hall was used as a Coast Guard Training Center in World War II and is said to be the birthplace of the Coast Guard Reserve.

Flagler's second wife, Ida Alice, was mentally unstable and spent the last years of her life in an institution. These days, she's seen lingering in the former hotel's halls and staring at its old paintings.

Flagler was known as a philanderer, and the ghost of one of his mistresses still roams the building. To keep his wife from finding out about the affair, Flagler locked the mistress away one too many times: She hanged herself from the chandelier in a room on the fourth floor, where her presence is still felt today. Students who later lived in that room heard screams.

If that trio isn't enough to scare you, look for two other ghosts. One is a pregnant woman in blue, who is believed to have been the mistress of a hotel guest. In despair over her situation, she ran up the stairs, tripped on her skirt, and broke her neck. And although the cause of his death is unknown, a spectral young boy has been seen wandering the premises. With all the paranormal activity in this building, one wonders how students get any work done there.

Riddles of the Riddle House

(West Palm Beach, Florida)

While functioning as a cemetery caretaker's home, West Palm Beach's Riddle House was always close to death. Since then, it's been relocated and repurposed, and now it sees its fair share of life—life after death, that is.

The "Painted Lady"

Built in 1905 as a gatekeeper's cottage, this pretty "Painted Lady" seemed incongruent with the cemetery it was constructed to oversee. Cloaked in grand Victorian finery, the house radiated the brightness of life. Perhaps that's what was intended: A cemetery caretaker's duties can be gloomy, so any bit of spirit lifting would likely be welcomed. Or so its builders thought. In the case of this particular house, however, "spirit lifting" took on a whole new meaning.

The first ghost sighted in the area was that of a former cemetery worker named Buck, who was killed during an argument with a townsperson. Shortly thereafter, Buck's ghost was seen doing chores around the cemetery and inside the cottage. Luckily, he seemed more interested in performing his duties than exacting revenge.

In the 1920s, the house received its current name when city manager Karl Riddle purchased it and took on the duty of overseeing the cemetery. During his tenure, a despondent employee named Joseph hung himself in the attic. This sparked a frenzy of paranormal phenomena inside the house, including the unexplained sounds of rattling chains and disembodied voices.

After Riddle moved out, the reports of paranormal activity slowed down—but such dormancy wouldn't last.

In 1995, the original Riddle House was torn down and relocated to the South Florida Fairgrounds' Yesteryear Village.

Traveling Spirits

By 1980, the Riddle House had fallen into disrepair and was abandoned. The city planned to demolish the building but instead decided to give it to John Riddle (Karl's nephew). He, in turn, donated it for preservation. The entire structure was moved—lock, stock, and barrel—to Yesteryear Village, a museum devoted to Florida's early years. There, it was placed on permanent display as an attractive token of days long past. There, too, its dark side would return—with a vengeance.

When workers began to reassemble the Riddle House, freshly awakened spirits kicked their antics into high gear. Ladders were tipped over, windows were smashed, and tools were thrown to the ground from the building's third floor. Workers were shocked when an unseen force threw a wooden board across a room, striking a carpenter in the head. The attacks were blamed on the spirit of Joseph, and the situation became so dangerous that work on the structure was halted for six months. After that, however, the Riddle House was restored to its previous glory.

The Riddle House was orignally built at 327 Acacia St. as a gatekeeper's cottage for Woodlawn Cemetery, the first cemetery in West Palm Beach, Florida.

Ghostly Unveiling

During the dedication of the Riddle House in the early 1980s, two unexpected guests showed up for the ceremony. Resplendent in Victorian garb, the couple added authenticity to the time period being celebrated. Many assumed that they were actors who were hired for the occasion; they were not. In fact, no one knew who they were. A few weeks later, century-old photos from the Riddle House were put on display. There, in sepia tones, stood the very same couple that guests had encountered during the dedication!

When the *Ghost Adventures* team spent a night locked inside the Riddle House in 2008, a medium warned the investigators that the spirit of Joseph is an evil entity that did not want them there. But that didn't stop investigator Zak Bagans from provoking the spirit. Bagans left a board at the top of the stairs and asked the entity to move it if it didn't want them there. Later, after the team heard footsteps in the room above them, the board fell down several stairs on its own. Throughout the course of the night, the team experienced unexplained noises and objects moving and falling by themselves. In the end, the researchers concluded that the Riddle House is definitely haunted and that whatever resides in the attic does not like men in particular, just as the medium had cautioned.

Ethereal stirrings at the Riddle House continue to this day. Unexplained sightings of a torso hanging in the attic window represent only part of the horror. And if history is any indicator, more supernatural sightings and activity are certainly to come.

Guest Ghosts Are the Norm at Austin's Driskill Hotel (Austin, Texas)

Southern hospitality abounds at the Driskill Hotel in downtown Austin, Texas. Built in 1886 by local cattle baron Colonel Jesse Lincoln Driskill, this lodging is hardly short on amenities. As a member of Historic Hotels of America and Associated Luxury Hotels International, the Driskill offers every comfort imaginable: From fancy linens and plasma-screen TVs to fine dining and complimentary shoeshines, this Austin institution has it all—including a few resident ghosts.

Meet the Ghosts

Considered one of the most haunted hotels in the United States, the Driskill is the eternal home of many spirits. First and foremost would have to be the ghost of Colonel Driskill himself. He makes his presence known by entering random guest rooms and smoking the cigars that he once loved so dearly. Driskill is also said to play with the lights in bathrooms, turning them on and off for fun.

Hotel guests and employees have seen water faucets turn on and off by themselves; some have even reported hearing the sound of noisy guests coming from an empty elevator. Others have felt as if they were being pushed out of bed, and some wake in the morning to find that their room's furniture has been rearranged during the night.

Since it opened, the Driskill has been a magnet for the rich and famous: Lyndon and Lady Bird Johnson had their first date at the hotel's restaurant, and Amelia Earhart, Louis Armstrong, and Richard Nixon have all sought respite there. At the Driskill, the upscale clientele mixes with the invisible guests that reside there full-time.

The Driskill was once known as "the finest hotel south of St. Louis," but today it is known more for its hauntings.

In the Spirit of Things

A more modern ghost that hangs around the Driskill is the "Houston Bride." When her fiancé called off their wedding plans in the 1990s, the young woman did what many other jilted brides would be tempted to do: She stole his credit cards and went shopping! She was last seen on the hotel elevator, loaded down with her packages. Retail therapy was apparently not the cure, however: She was found dead a few days later, the victim of a gunshot wound to the abdomen. Some guests have seen her apparition with her arms full of packages; others have spotted her in her wedding gown. Oddly, it seems to be those guests who are at the hotel for weddings or bachelorette parties that are most likely to see her. And even stranger, some brides consider it good luck to catch a glimpse of the tragic "Houston Bride" before their own weddings. Maybe she counts as something blue.

Jesse Driskill financed the construction of the hotel with enormous amounts of cash he earned from supplying beef to the Confederates during the Civil War.

A Ghost With Fashion Sense

When singer Annie Lennox stayed at the Driskill Hotel in the 1980s while performing in Austin, she laid out two dresses to consider after she got out of the shower. When she emerged from the bathroom, only one dress was still on the bed; the other was once again hanging in the closet.

A ghost dressed in Victorian-era clothing has been seen at night where the front desk used to stand, and guests have detected the scent of roses in the area. This is believed to be the spirit of Mrs. Bridges, who worked at the Driskill as a front-desk clerk in the early 1900s.

The spirit of a young girl haunts the lobby on the first floor; she is believed to have been the daughter of a senator. In 1887, she was chasing a ball on the grand staircase when she tripped and fell to her death. Today, her ghost is often heard laughing and bouncing a ball up and down those same stairs.

The spirit of Peter J. Lawless might still be residing in Room 419, where he lived from 1886 until 1916 or 1917. Although the housekeeping crew cleans and vacuums that room like all the others, they often report finding rumpled bedclothes, open dresser drawers, and footprints in the bathroom—after they've already cleaned the room. Lawless is typically blamed for this mischievous behavior, and his specter is also often spotted near the elevators on the fifth floor. He pauses to check his watch when the doors open—then he promptly disappears.

Fort Worth Stockyards
(Fort Worth, Texas)

The spirits haunting the Fort Worth Stockyards are well aware they are in Texas, because they have made their hauntings as prominent as possible—exactly as state custom requires!

The Stockyards used to have quite a few head of beef, but now they mostly have tourists. Today the Fort Worth Stockyards are a historic district (or a tourist trap, depending on perspective) like Vancouver's Gastown or Wichita's Cowtown. Fort Worthians revel in the ghosty spice that seasons the Stockyards' history. For a slight fee, some will take you on a tour. Here are some of the highlights.

Good Golly...

One of the Stockyards' most famous haunted spots is Miss Molly's Hotel, formerly a boarding house, speakeasy and bordello. Seven themed and named rooms are lush with all the attendant décor you'd expect. The Cattleman's and Cowboy's rooms are notorious for ghost sightings. Most commonly, the apparitions look like young women, perhaps the spirits of past 'soiled doves' who too often came to grief in the old West. One modern housekeeper quit after extra coins kept appearing after she'd already collected her tips!

The Fort Worth Stockyards were a very important part of America's cattle industry from 1890 to 1950. The Fort Worth Union Stockyards opened following the arrival of the railway in the city in 1876. By 1907, the stockyards were selling a million cattle a year. Business began to suffer for the stockyards in the mid-20th century due to cattle auctions being held closer to where the cattle were raised.

Today, the stockyards are an entertainment and tourism district filled with clubs, bars, and dining. They are the last standing stockyards in the U.S.

Cantina Cadillac

This hopping night spot is so haunted that at night, it always has at least two staffers. Tills are often short or over, with the shortage or overage made up the next day. This could just be human error, except that it happens here suspiciously more often than in most establishments. One day, while closing out downstairs, the Cantina crew heard noise topside. They went up to find all the furniture shoved into the middle of the dance floor. Clever prank or ghost? We don't know.

Maverick Building

It has seen many uses, including its current incarnation as a western apparel store. Of old, the Maverick was a saloon, and reputedly Bonnie Parker's (as in Bonnie and Clyde) favorite gambling joint. The ghost upstairs is believed to be female, probably hailing from the brothel days of the early 20th century. Even when the Stockyards mostly smelled of cattle, and what goes into and comes out of them, one could smell roses upstairs. Years back, someone experimented by leaving a bouquet of roses upstairs. She came back later to find them tastefully distributed throughout the rooms.

Cattlemen's Steakhouse

Would you like some spirits with your enormous medium rare rib eye? Can do, if you can get staff to take you downstairs at the Cattlemen's—they go in pairs. Disembodied voices call their names, doors open and close unattended, and stuff gets moved around at random. Ghost hunters have bagged some nice orb photos here, and an actual ghost photo adorns the upstairs wall—an odd face behind a bolo-hat-wearing mortal.

White Elephant Saloon

In the old days, this was one of the rougher and sleazier drunkeries, and was in a different location. When that old structure crumbled, owners moved all the memorabilia here with the name. It seems that the unseen inhabitants came along, or were perhaps already in residence. Three violent deaths have occurred in the basement of the current building, leaving it with a creepy sensation. As with many hauntings, the staff describe glasses and implements mysteriously moving to new locations.

Remember the Alamo!
(San Antonio, Texas)

While no one knows for certain why ghosts choose particular places to haunt, one explanation suggests that many earthbound spirits are victims of tragedy. One of the greatest tragedies in American history occurred when General Santa Anna's Mexican army slaughtered nearly 200 Texans during the Battle of the Alamo. The tales of those gallant men who refused to give up the mission-turned-fortress still resonate with us today. In fact, it seems as though many of those brave souls haven't left.

Standing Their Ground

In early February 1836, the fledgling government of Texas was in disarray, and its army couldn't muster much in the way of reinforcements. As a result, when Colonel James Bowie, Colonel William Travis, and Davy Crockett arrived in San Antonio, they knew that little help was on the way, so their scant garrison of around 180 soldiers prepared to face a Mexican army of more than 1,800.

General Santa Anna shelled the mission for twelve days before ordering his men to charge. The brave soldiers inside the fort were hopelessly outnumbered, but they fought valiantly, killing or wounding hundreds of Mexican soldiers. The battle was over in less than ninety minutes, and only a handful of the fighting Texans survived (they were later executed), along with the women and children who Santa Anna spared from the slaughter.

General Santa Anna was a Mexican military leader and politician. He fought in the Texas Revolution and Mexican-American War and also served as Mexican president twice in his lifetime.

The Battle of the Alamo has become so famous in the lore of American history that the fact the Alamo was built by the Spanish to serve as a Catholic mission for Native Americans is almost completely forgotten.

Protective Phantoms

Several weeks after the fateful battle took place, Santa Anna ordered his men to raze the Alamo, thus erasing any evidence of the Texans' brave stand. The task fell to Colonel Sanchez, who rode with his men to dismantle the old church. As they set about their task, however, six phantom monks appeared from the walls of the Alamo. The monks, armed with flaming swords, made their demands clear. "Do not touch the walls of the Alamo!" the spirits shrieked. Colonel Sanchez and his men—frightened for their lives and their very souls—retreated to camp to report to General Andrade. The general was not impressed by the story, so he brought a contingent of soldiers and a cannon back to the mission to finish the job himself. No sooner had he ordered the cannon aimed at the chapel door than the monks appeared again. Armed with their flaming swords and screaming their singular demand, they startled the troops and spooked their horses. General Andrade was thrown from his mount, and when he regained control of his horse, he turned his attention back to the Alamo. It was then that a wall of fire appeared to erupt from the ground, preventing him from getting any closer to the mission. To his further horror, the thick black smoke produced by the fire quickly took the form of a large man with a ball of fire in each of his spectral hands. The general ran and never returned, but this was only the beginning of the Alamo's supernatural history.

Colonel James Bowie is famous today in Texas as a folk hero and pioneer, who played a large role in the Texas Revolution. He was killed on March 6th, 1862, with the rest of the defenders of the Alamo. When told of her son's death, Bowie's mother said, "I'll wager no wounds were found in his back."

Guarding Ghosts

In the years after the Battle of the Alamo, the fort was used as a jail. During this time, newspapers reported sightings of a sentry patrolling the roof. The guard was spotted walking east to west and back again each night; however, the authorities claimed that they'd never stationed a man there. In fact, anyone who bothered to watch the guard for more than a moment noticed that he quickly vanished. Most guards and officers refused to patrol the building at night because they kept hearing horrible moans in the darkness. It sounded as if a soldier's final moments—perhaps being stabbed to death by bayonet-wielding Mexican soldiers—were being reenacted over and over again each night. The men also reported feeling as though eyes were following them throughout the building. This ominous presence seems to stalk visitors to the Alamo to this day.

Wandering Wraiths

The spirits guarding the Alamo aren't the only specters that make themselves known at the site. Visitors often report seeing a young blond-haired boy in a window over what is now a gift shop. Every year in early March, near the anniversary of the massacre, neighbors say that a horse can be heard galloping on the pavement at dawn; perhaps it's a spectral courier who is still trying to reach Colonel Travis. Artilleryman Anthony Wolfe's young sons, who died at the hands of the Mexican army like their father, are said to go along on the daily tours of the Alamo: Many tour groups have reported seeing the two young boys following them and have noted that the boys vanish when the groups reach the chapel. Park rangers have also seen a man dressed in period clothing; when they followed him across the grounds, he faded from view when he reached the chapel.

The attack on the Alamo came in three waves, with the last leading to the defenders retreating into the interior of the building as the Mexicans began to scale the walls. There are reports that some five to seven defenders surrendered to the Mexican army and were executed immediately. Eyewitness accounts record somewhere between 182 and 257 Texans dying, and around 600 Mexicans.

This is the only known drawing of William B. Travis to be done during his lifetime. Travis originally thought he might disobey his orders when he was assigned to raise a company of soldiers to help reinforce the besieged Texans at the Alamo, writing, "I am willing, nay anxious, to go to the defense of Bexar, but sir, I am unwilling to risk my reputation . . . by going off into the enemy's country with such little means, so few men, and with them so badly equipped." Travis eventually obeyed his orders and fought till his death.

Celebrity Specters

Not all the ghosts at the Alamo are unknown figures. One spirit that is often spotted on the grounds wears a buckskin shirt, moccasins, and a coonskin cap. Sometimes he stands at attention, a flintlock rifle at his side; other times he's leaning on a wall near the chapel, dying from his wounds. One ranger even claimed that he got close enough to determine that it was definitely Davy Crockett and that he watched as phantom soldiers in Mexican uniforms attacked the famed frontiersman. Multiple people have even reported seeing Crockett from different vantage points at the same time.

Finally, there's the case of John Wayne, who became obsessed with the old mission while he was directing his epic western *The Alamo* (1960) on location. Since his death in 1979, "The Duke" has been spotted at the Alamo on more than one occasion. He usually just wanders the grounds, but occasionally he is seen conversing with the other restless spirits. If John Wayne did indeed choose to haunt the Alamo, he certainly has plenty of company.

The bodies of the Texan defenders were burned in a pyre on site by the Mexican Army. It is said that Juan Seguin returned to the site a few weeks later, collected a handful of ashes and put them in a small coffin marked with the names Travis, Crockitt, and Bowie, and then buried the coffin under a peach grove. The location of the burial site has never been found.

There is controversy over Davy Crockett's fate at the Alamo. Although it is certain that he died at the Alamo, it is uncertain whether or not Crockett was one of the defenders who surrendered to Santa Anna's army. Many believe this rumor was made to continue Santa Anna's villainous depiction in history.

Ghosts of Higher Education
(Various)

Colleges and universities are some of the oldest institutions in America, so it's not surprising that they might harbor ghosts of those who passed through their hallowed halls in times past. College buildings and their surrounding grounds are often home to eternal residents that give new meaning to the term school spirit.

Eastern Illinois University
(Charleston, Illinois)

The resident ghost of Eastern Illinois University's Pemberton Hall was a young woman who was brutally raped and murdered there by a school custodian in 1917. Fortunately for current students, the fourth floor—where the crime took place—has been closed off for years, but maintenance workers still report seeing bloody footprints appear and then disappear on that floor. Residents elsewhere in the dormitory have heard piano music coming from the vacant floor above, where the murdered coed is said to play her spirited song.

Harvard University
(Cambridge, Massachusetts)

Harvard's Thayer Hall—which was once used as a textile mill—is now inhabited by ghosts of years past. Spirits dressed in Victorian apparel have been seen entering and exiting through doors that no longer exist. Perhaps they're seeking the warmth of the building because they are often seen during the winter months.

Huntingdon College (Montgomery, Alabama)

If you visit Pratt Hall at Huntingdon College in Montgomery, Alabama, you might just encounter the ghost of a young lady named Martha. Better known today as the "Red Lady," Martha left her native New York and enrolled at Huntingdon (then called the Women's College of Alabama) in the early 1900s because it was her grandmother's alma mater. She was known on campus for her love of red: She decorated her room with red drapes and a red rug, and she often wore red dresses. Lonely and taunted by her peers, Martha killed herself in despair. She now haunts Pratt Hall, where residents occasionally catch a glimpse of a young lady dressed in red. In recent years, she seems to have gotten bolder, as students have reported cold blasts of air surrounding those who are caught picking on their classmates.

Kenyon College (Gambier, Ohio)

Established in 1824, Kenyon is one of Ohio's most haunted colleges. At least three students who committed suicide in different dormitories now haunt them: One rearranges furniture in Manning Hall; one turns off lights, knocks on doors, and flushes toilets in Lewis Hall; and one roams around Norton Hall late at night. And back when Bolton Dance Studio was known as "The Greenhouse" (so named because of the building's glass roof) and housed the college pool, swimmers would occasionally hear a voice calling out to them. More recently, dancers have seen wet footprints in the studio, heard splashing sounds, and observed showers in the locker room turn on and off when no one is present. These strange occurrences are attributed to the "Greenhouse Ghost," which is thought to be the spirit of a male student who died at the pool in a diving accident during the 1940s.

Luther College (Decorah, Iowa)

The ghost of Gertrude—a Decorah high school student who desperately wanted to attend Luther College back in the days before women students were admitted there—is said to make her presence known at Larsen Hall. Students living there have blamed Gertrude for walking the halls at all hours of the night, sounding the fire alarm, and stealing items—especially modern lingerie—and sometimes leaving behind her own old-fashioned garments. She was killed in 1918 when she was hit by a car while riding her bicycle, ending her collegiate dreams before they even started.

St. Joseph's College (Emmitsburg, Maryland)

In 1810, Mother Elizabeth Seton, a Catholic nun, founded St. Joseph's Academy and Free School for Catholic girls. In 1902, the school became St. Joseph's College until it closed entirely in 1973. Mother Seton was buried on campus and was canonized in 1975. Today, her ghost is often seen gliding through the hallways of the school she knew so well. Observers have seen her walking with the ghost of an unidentified doctor who carries a medical bag, both apparently still searching for suffering souls to heal.

University of Notre Dame (South Bend, Indiana)

The hallowed halls of Notre Dame are home to several ghosts, including Father Edward Sorin, the university's founder, who is said to wander all over the campus, including in the Main Building and near the famous golden dome. Native Americans from the Potawatomi tribe are thought to haunt Columba Hall, which is located between the two campus lakes—on land where they once lived and buried their dead. In addition, Washington Hall is rumored to be the home of a few ghosts, among them a steeplejack who fell to his death in 1886 and Brother Canute Lardner, who died peacefully while watching a movie there in 1946. And then, of course, there's the ghost of George Gipp, Notre Dame's famous football star. Gipp died of pneumonia and strep throat, which he may have contracted after spending the night on Washington Hall's front steps because he stayed out after curfew and was locked out of the dorm. On his deathbed, he allegedly told coach Knute Rockne that when his players need a pep talk, he should tell them to "win one for the Gipper." Since Gipp's death in 1920, students have heard unexplained footsteps, doors slamming, and ghostly music in Washington Hall.

Father Edward Sorin was offered land from the Bishop of Vincennes in 1842 on the condition that he build a college on the site within two years. He arrived in Indiana from France with eight Holy Cross brothers on November 26, 1842, and began a school in the old log chapel of Father Stephen Badin. Soon after he built the Old College, the first main building, and the first church with two students under his tutelage.

San Jose State University (San Jose, California)

San Jose was one of the U.S. cities where Japanese Americans were told to report for assignment to internment camps during World War II. It was in the old campus gymnasium at San Jose State that these people gathered for processing before they were sent to their new "homes." So it's really no surprise that ghostly voices have been heard crying and speaking in a foreign language at the gym. Students there have also heard footsteps and doors closing when no one else is present.

Conneaut Lake Park's Thrill Seeking Ghosts (Conneaut Lake, Pennsylvania)

Conneaut Lake Park, which is located about thirty miles south of Lake Erie, opened in 1892 as Exposition Park on the western shore of the deep glacial lake that shares its name. The park became so popular that several hotels sprang up nearby to accommodate the crowds. Conneaut Lake Park still features many quaint, refurbished old rides that evoke the laid-back atmosphere of the lakeside area's past.

The wooden-tracked Blue Streak, which opened in 1937, where a rider allegedly died, is a prime example of how the past still lives in the park.

The Conneaut Lake Park was built on land once owned by Aaron Lynce, who used the land as a boat landing for Lake Conneaut. Col. Frank Mantor bought the land from Lynce to open a permanent fairground and exposition site for livestock, machinery, and other industrial products coming out in that day and age. Mantor built a dance and convention hall, a bathhouse, and a hotel (which was built from the old farmhouse on the property).

The Burning Bride

In 1943, a large section of the Hotel Conneaut burned and spawned the park's most famous ghost: "Elizabeth," the phantom bride. According to local lore, Elizabeth was a hotel guest who perished in the fire after her groom was unable to save her. Although historians have not found evidence that this actually happened, the spirit seems to remain in an eternal holding pattern, waiting to be rescued from the flames. A hint of jasmine-scented perfume is often the first clue that Elizabeth is near.

Many guests have reported seeing the apparition of a young woman wearing a 1940s-era dress gliding silently around the hotel. Sometimes she emerges from a solid wall that at one time was a hallway opening; she seems to be confused regarding her whereabouts. Occasionally, she is spotted waltzing with her groom on the front veranda.

The park's first mechanical ride, a carousel, premiered in 1899. Other rides and a midway were soon added to the list of the park's entertainment options, including the Figure Eight roller coaster debuting in 1902.

Hotel Horrors

Another ghost at the hotel is the spirit of Angelina, a young girl who was allegedly killed in a fatal tricycle accident on the hotel's balcony or stairs. According to an article in the *Meadville Tribune*, spiritual medium Kitty Osborne saw the tiny trikester pedaling down a hallway just outside her room. Osborne told the *Tribune* that she was "flabbergasted" at the sight.

The *Tribune* also interviewed George Deshner, the park's general manager, who said that he and many other employees have had brushes with unknown forces in the hotel. On several occasions, staff members have checked to make sure that all of the hotel's windows are closed and locked for the night only to discover later that one had mysteriously reopened. Lights turn on and off by themselves, and the manager himself has felt unseen hands shove him against a wall.

Even the hotel restaurant harbors its own spook: a chef dressed in spotless whites with an old-fashioned bow tied around his neck. He is said to move brooms and garbage cans, and guests have reported seeing him staring at them through the restaurant's window after the eatery is locked up for the night. One group of women observed the otherworldly figure writing on a piece of paper. Perhaps he was planning the next day's dessert specials: booberry pie and sheet cake!

A scene from the 1909 Conneaut Lake Fair.

Gettysburg's Ghosts
(Gettysburg, Pennsylvania)

The Battle of Gettysburg holds a unique and tragic place in the annals of American history. It was the turning point of the Civil War and its bloodiest battle. From July 1 through July 3, 1863, both the Union and Confederate armies amassed a total of more than 50,000 casualties (including dead, wounded, and missing) at the Battle of Gettysburg. All that bloodshed and suffering is said to have permanently stained Gettysburg and left the entire area brimming with ghosts. It is often cited as one of the most haunted places in America.

First Ghostly Sighting

Few people realize that the first sighting of a ghost at Gettysburg allegedly took place before the battle was over. As the story goes, Union reinforcements from the 20th Maine Infantry were nearing Gettysburg but became lost as they traveled in the dark. As the regiment reached a fork in the road, they were greeted by a man wearing a three-cornered hat, who was sitting atop a horse. Both the man and his horse appeared to be glowing. The man, who bore a striking resemblance to George Washington, motioned for the regiment to follow. Believing the man to be a Union general, Colonel Joshua Chamberlain ordered his regiment to follow the man. Just about the time Chamberlain starting thinking there was something odd about the helpful stranger, the man simply vanished.

As the regiment searched for him, they suddenly realized they had been led to Little Round Top—the very spot where, the following day, the 20th Maine Infantry would repel a Confederate advance in one of the turning points of the Battle of Gettysburg. To his dying day, Chamberlain, as well as the roughly 100 men who saw the spectral figure that night, believed that they had been led to Little Round Top by the ghost of George Washington himself.

The Battle of Gettysburg was the most deadly battle for both the Confederacy and Union. The horrific three days of battle in July of 1862 still linger on the battlefield today.

The 20th Maine Volunteer Infantry Regiment successfully defended their position on top Little Round Top on July 2, 1862. The engagement ended with the Union's downhill bayonet charge that still resonates in the halls of military history today.

Devil's Den

A lot of mystery surrounds this photo because some say that it was hoaxed by Alexander Gardner. This photo, "The Home of a Rebel Sharpshooter," supposedly contains the same body as another Gardner photo, "A Sharpshooter's Last Sleep," which has led many to claim that this photo was staged.

At the base of Little Round Top and across a barren field lies an outcropping of rocks known as Devil's Den. It was from this location that Confederate sharpshooters took up positions and fired at the Union soldiers stationed along Little Round Top. Eventually, Union soldiers followed the telltale sign of gun smoke and picked off the sharpshooters one by one.

After Devil's Den was secured by Union forces, famous Civil War photographer Alexander Gardner was allowed to come in and take photos of the area. One of his most famous pictures, "The Home of a Rebel Sharpshooter," was taken at Devil's Den and shows a Confederate sharpshooter lying dead near the rocks. There was only one problem: The photograph was staged. Gardner apparently dragged a dead Confederate soldier over from another location and positioned the body himself. Legend has it that the ghost of the Confederate soldier was unhappy with how his body was treated, so his ghost often causes cameras in Devil's Den to malfunction.

Pickett's Charge

On July 3, the final day of the battle, Confederate General Robert E. Lee felt the battle slipping away from him, and in what many saw as an act of desperation, ordered 12,000 Confederate soldiers to attack the Union forces who were firmly entrenched on Cemetery Ridge. During the attack, known as Pickett's Charge, the Confederates slowly and methodically marched across open fields toward the heavily fortified Union lines. The attack failed miserably, with more than 6,000 Confederate soldiers killed or wounded before they retreated. The defeat essentially signaled the beginning of the end of the Civil War.

Today, it is said that if you stand on top of Cemetery Ridge and look out across the field, you might catch a glimpse of row after ghostly row of Confederate soldiers slowly marching toward their doom at the hands of Union soldiers.

Alexander Gardner's "A Sharpshooter's Last Sleep."

Jennie Wade

While the battle was raging near Cemetery Ridge, twenty-year-old Mary Virginia "Ginnie" Wade (also known as Jennie Wade) was at her sister's house baking bread for the Union troops stationed nearby. Without warning, a stray bullet flew through the house, struck the young woman, and killed her instantly, making her the only civilian known to die during the Battle of Gettysburg. Visitors to the historical landmark known as the Jennie Wade house often report catching a whiff of freshly baked bread. Jennie's spirit is also felt throughout the house, especially in the basement, where her body was placed until relatives could bury her when there was a break in the fighting.

Cemetery Hill was a major stategic location for the Union to set up an artillery line. This photo was taken in July 1862, just after the Battle of Gettysburg.

The Battle of Gettysburg was the deadliest battle in the Civil War with both army's casualties estimated from 46,000 to 51,000 soldiers. The Union suffered around 23,000 casualties while the Confederate losses are much harder to calculate.

Farnsworth House

Though it was next to impossible to determine who fired the shot that killed Jennie Wade, it is believed that it came from the attic of the Farnsworth house. Now operating as a bed-and-breakfast, during the Battle of Gettysburg the building was taken over by Confederate sharpshooters. One in particular, the one who may have fired the shot that killed Jennie Wade, is said to have holed himself up in the attic. No one knows for sure because the sharpshooter didn't survive the battle, but judging by the dozens of bullet holes and scars along the sides of the Farnsworth house, he didn't go down without a fight. Perhaps that's why his ghost is still lingering—to let us know what really happened in the Farnsworth attic. Passersby often report looking up at the attic window facing the Jennie Wade house and seeing a ghostly figure looking down at them.

Aside from being the deadliest battle of the Civil War, the Battle of Gettysburg saw the highest number of generals killed in battle during the war.

Pennsylvania Hall at Gettysburg College

One of the most frightening ghost stories associated with the Battle of Gettysburg was originally told to author Mark Nesbitt. The story centers around Gettysburg College's Pennsylvania Hall, which the basement was turned into a makeshift hospital. Late one night in the early 1980s, two men who were working on an upper floor got on the elevator and pushed the button for the first floor. But as the elevator descended, it passed the first floor and continued to the basement. Upon reaching the basement, the elevator doors opened. One look was all the workers needed to realize that they had somehow managed to travel back in time. The familiar surroundings of the basement had been replaced by bloody, screaming Confederate soldiers on stretchers. Doctors stood over the soldiers, feverishly trying to save their lives. Blood and gore were everywhere.

As the two men started frantically pushing the elevator buttons, some of the doctors began walking toward them. Without a second to spare, the elevator doors closed just as the ghostly figures reached them. This time the elevator rose to the first floor and opened, revealing modern-day furnishings. Despite repeated return visits to the basement, nothing out of the ordinary has ever been reported again.

Spangler's Spring

As soon as the Battle of Gettysburg was over, soldiers began relating their personal experiences to local newspapers. One story that spread quickly centered on the cooling waters of Spangler's Spring. It was said that at various times during the fierce fighting, both sides agreed to periodic ceasefires so that Union and Confederate soldiers could stand side-by-side and drink from the spring. It's a touching story, but in all likelihood, it never actually happened. Even if it did, it doesn't explain the ghostly woman in a white dress who is seen at the spring. Some claim that the "Woman in White" is the spirit of a woman who lost her lover during the Battle of Gettysburg. Another theory is that she was a young woman who took her own life after breaking up with her lover years after the war ended.

Because of Pennsylvania Hall's position in relation to the Battle of Gettysburg, both Union and Confederate sides used the building to send signals from their signal corps and to tend to their injured soldiers.

Penance for Your Sins
(Philadelphia, Pennsylvania)

The remains of the Eastern State Penitentiary—the location of a truly unique experiment in the history of law enforcement—stand on what is now Fairmount Avenue in Philadelphia. Designed by John Haviland, the facility was different from other prisons in that it was meant to stress reform rather than punishment. It was thought that by giving a prisoner plenty of time to reflect on his wrongdoing, he would eventually reform himself by turning to God to make penance—hence the word *penitentiary*.

In October 1829, when the Eastern State Penitentiary officially opened, it was one of the largest public buildings of its kind in the United States. And after its front gates swung open, its unique features blew prisoners and employees away. For starters, the entire complex resembled a giant wagon wheel, with seven wings of cells emerging from the center like spokes. The hallways themselves looked like the vestibules of a church.

Over the years, changes were enacted in an attempt to remedy the Eastern State Penitentiary's cruel environment, but none helped. Finally, in 1971, the penitentiary was officially closed. In the mid-1990s, after sitting abandoned for years, the building was reopened for tours.

Isolation and Madness

Individual cells were designed to house only one inmate each. The idea was that prisoners needed time to reflect on what they had done wrong, and giving them cell mates would only distract them from doing that.

The only people with whom inmates were allowed to interact on a regular basis were the warden—who visited every prisoner once a day—and the guards—who served meals and brought inmates to and from their cells. Inmates were permitted to go outside for exercise, but they could only do that alone. When an inmate was removed from his cell for any reason, he was required to wear a hood. Prisoners were to remain silent at all times unless asked a direct question by prison personnel; failure to adhere to this rule meant swift, sadistic punishment.

Torturous Behavior

The facility's initial intent may have been to get inmates to understand that they needed to follow the rules in order to be reformed, but that quickly broke down into brutality by the guards and officials. Minor offenses, including making even the smallest noise, were often enough for authorities to subject inmates to a series of hellish punishments. Restraint devices such as straitjackets and the "mad chair"—a chair equipped with so many restraints that it made even the slightest movement impossible—were often employed. If an inmate was caught talking, he might be forced to wear the "iron gag"—a piece of metal that was clamped to his tongue while the other end was attached to leather gloves that he was forced to wear; movement resulted in excruciating pain. Legend has it that several prisoners accidentally severed their own tongues while wearing the iron gag, and at least one died while wearing the device.

Another method of torture utilized at the Eastern State Pen was the water bath. Inmates were tied to the penitentiary walls and doused with freezing water, even in the middle of winter; under the most extreme conditions, the water would freeze on the inmates' bodies.

Perhaps one of the most heinous means of punishing an inmate was to place him in the "Klondike." While other prisons have "The Hole"—which is essentially solitary confinement—the Klondike at the Eastern State Pen was a group of four subterranean cells without windows or plumbing; inmates were made to live down there—often for several weeks at a time.

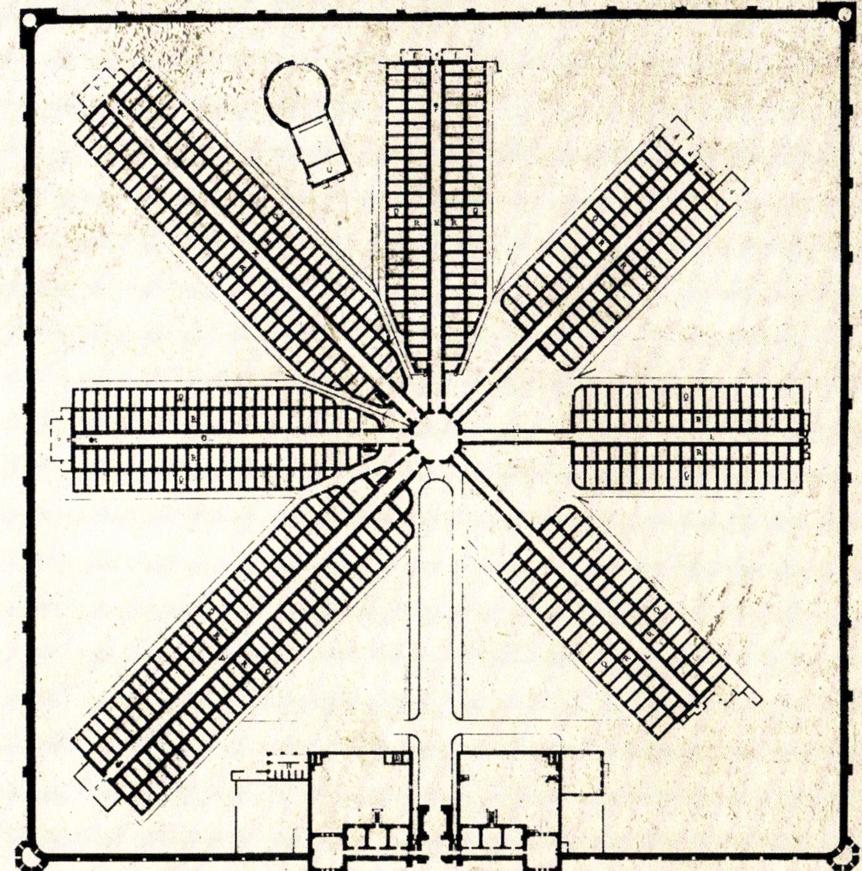

The 1836 floor plan on the penitentiary. A hub-and-spoke layout allowed for constant surveillance from the central guard tower at the center of the hub.

It is said that the idea to build such a large and intimidating penitentiary first originated from a meeting held at Benjamin Franklin's house in 1787. Eastern State Penitentiary architect John Haviland was most inspired by the designs of prisons and asylums built in Ireland and England during the 1780s.

Swift Decline

The Eastern State Penitentiary was designed to change the world of incarceration in a positive way, but it failed miserably. In fact, when British author Charles Dickens visited the United States in 1842, one of the places that he wanted to see was the Eastern State Pen. From across the Atlantic, Dickens had heard about the marvelous and unique penitentiary and wanted to see it for himself. He was shocked by what he witnessed there, calling it "hopeless… cruel, and wrong."

Al Capone's cell in Cellblock 8. Capone was sent to Eastern State Penitentiary after being charged for faking an illness to avoid a court hearing. He spent nearly a year in this cell.

When it comes to paranormal activity, Cellblock 12 is a very active area in the penitentiary.

Not All Who Walk These Blocks Are Among the Living…

Looking back at the tortuous history of the Eastern State Pen, it should come as no surprise that more than a few ghosts can be found there. In fact, records indicate that inmates reported paranormal activity on the premises as early as the 1940s, so it seems that ghosts were in residence there long before the prison closed. Perhaps that explains what happened to locksmith Gary Johnson while he was working on a lock during a restoration of the prison in the early 1990s. After Johnson popped the door open, he saw shadowy shapes moving all around him. It was as if he'd allowed all the ghosts to once again roam free.

If there's one area of the penitentiary where visitors are most likely to experience paranormal activity, it is Cellblock 12. Many people have reported hearing voices echoing throughout the cellblock and even laughter coming from the cells themselves. Shadow figures are also seen in abundance there.

Another location at the Eastern State Penitentiary that is said to be haunted is the guard tower that sits high atop the main wall. People standing outside the prison have seen a shadowy figure walking along the wall; it calmly looks down at them from time to time.

The central guard tower watched over the original seven cellblocks. At the time it was built, the general philosophy of the prison was not just to punish the prisoner but to lead them to a new spiritual life. Many believed that the rules of silence that were enforced among inmates and guards would allow the inmates to reflect on their ugly crimes and behaviors, making them become “genuinely penitent” Hence the new meaning of the word *penitentiary* that took at that time.

Dude, Run!

Over the years, various ghost-hunting television shows have visited the Eastern State Penitentiary and submitted paranormal evidence to their viewers. The facility was featured in a 2001 episode of MTV's *Fear*. In 2007, *Most Haunted* investigated the place, and *Ghost Adventures* filmed an episode there in 2009. But if the Eastern State Penitentiary is forever linked to a paranormal research show, it would be *Ghost Hunters,* due to its team's 2004 investigation and the actions of one of its members.

At approximately 3 a.m., investigator Brian Harnois of The Atlantic Paranormal Society (TAPS) entered Cellblock 4 with Dave Hobbs, a member of the show's production crew. As Hobbs snapped a photograph, he and Harnois thought they saw a huge black shape rise up and move in front of them. They both panicked, and Harnois yelled out the now-famous line, “Dude, run!” after which the pair bolted down the hallway, much to the chagrin of their fellow investigators (who quickly deduced that the shape had been caused by the camera flash). The incident overshadowed an intriguing piece of evidence that was captured later that night, when one of the team's video cameras recorded a dark shape—almost human in form—that appeared to be moving quickly along a cellblock. Try as they might, TAPS was unable to come up with a scientific explanation for the shape, leaving who or what it was open to interpretation.

The Eastern State Penitentiary had running water, flushing toilets, and heat during the winter, which was more than what the recently completed White House in Washington boasted.

West Point's Spirited Residents

(West Point, New York)

The Pickpocket Poltergeist

In October 1972, demonologists Ed and Lorraine Warren were invited to give a lecture at West Point. While they were there, they were asked to investigate some paranormal activity that had been occurring at the superintendent's house. It seems that, among other things, personal items and wallets of guests had come up missing…only to be discovered later, neatly arranged on the dresser in the master bedroom.

Lorraine was able to communicate with the "Pickpocket Poltergeist," who identified himself as a man named Greer. In the early 1800s, he had been wrongly accused of murder, and although he was ultimately exonerated, he was anguishing in sorrow and was unable to move on. Lorraine urged him to go into the light.

The United States Military Academy at West Point has an illustrious history. Since 1802, it has educated young men (and women, beginning in 1976) preparing to serve their country as officers in the U.S. Army; prior to that time, West Point was a military fort. With that much history, it's no surprise that these hallowed halls are home to a ghost or two.

A cranky Irish cook named Molly is thought to haunt the superintendent's mansion (seen here), where she once worked. "Miss Molly"—as she was called when she lived there in the early 19th century—was the maid of Brigadier General Sylvanus Thayer. A hard worker even in death, Molly is often seen kneading bread in the mansion's kitchen.

Back in the 1920s, a spirit inhabiting Officer's Quarters 107B (seen here) on Professor's Row had to be exorcised. It is unknown whether this was a malevolent ghost or a demonic force, but whatever it was and whatever it did, it frightened two servant girls so terribly that they ran out of the house screaming in the middle of the night.

Room 4714

But it is Room 4714 in the 47th Division Barracks that has caused the most supernatural speculation. Paranormal activity was first reported there shortly after the Warrens' visit, when students Art Victor and James O'Connor shared the room. One day, when O'Connor went to take a shower, he noticed that his bathrobe was swinging back and forth—but nothing was blowing it. Then suddenly, the temperature in the room dropped several degrees.

A couple of days later, O'Connor saw an apparition of a soldier wearing a uniform and carrying a musket. The following evening, both boys felt an extreme drop in temperature and then saw a man's upper body float through the room; it hovered between the floor and ceiling for a few minutes before disappearing.

One night shortly thereafter, two fellow cadets—Keith Bakken and Terry Meehan—volunteered to spend the night in Room 4714. During the night, Meehan awoke and caught a glimpse of a ghostly figure near the ceiling. By the time Bakken woke up, the apparition was gone, but both boys experienced an extreme drop in temperature. After the campus newspaper published an article about the strange activity, several other cadets offered to sleep in the room. A thermocouple was used to scientifically measure any temperature changes. The coldest temperature was always found right next to O'Connor. Oddly, one night when other cadets were in his room waiting for the ghost, O'Connor saw the specter in another room while the boys in Room 4714 saw nothing.

Although a significant number of cadets saw the apparition and felt the drastic temperature change in Room 4714, the identity of this spirit remains unknown.

The 47th Division Barracks are located near the site of a disastrous house fire that killed an officer. The building is also close to a graveyard in which some Revolutionary War-era soldiers are buried. Could the ghost be one of these military men attempting to bond with the new breed of cadet? If so, the spirit eventually gave up—it hasn't been seen or felt since the 1970s.

Sleepless at the Empire State Building (Manhattan, New York)

Located in the center of Manhattan, the Empire State Building represents financial success as well as architectural beauty, but it wasn't always that way. The Art Deco building opened in 1931, during the Great Depression when times were tough. You'd never know that now, however, as the building bustles with activity. Workers, sweethearts, families, and tourists are all attracted to the structure, and with all the activity that has taken place within its walls—especially on the observation deck—it's no wonder that a few spirits have lingered.

As an international icon, the 102-story Empire State Building welcomes visitors from all over the world every day. In fact, it is estimated that 110 million people have made trips to the top of the revered skyscraper.

What Makes a Ghost a Ghost?

Throughout the history of the Empire State Building, numerous people have died there of natural causes. Others may have passed away elsewhere but returned to haunt the building because it held a special place in their hearts in life: Perhaps they worked there or met their spouse there and wanted to spend a little more time there—maybe eternity.

The process of building a skyscraper of this size can also produce a few ghosts. Official records document only five deaths related to the construction of the Empire State Building, but you can be sure that some of those workers have remained to see the finished project.

In addition, on July 28, 1945, a ten-ton B-25 bomber headed for Newark encountered fog and visibility problems. Just before 10 a.m., the plane crashed into the seventy-ninth floor of the Empire State Building, killing eleven office workers and three crew members.

Of the five deaths that happened on site before the building's completion, one death was the suicide of a worker who had been laid off.

Choosing the Afterlife

Over the years, many people who have fallen on hard times have gone to the Empire State Building to end their lives: The structure has been the site of at least thirty suicides. Due to the violent nature of such deaths, suicide victims probably account for most of the unsettled spirits found there. Although several suicide attempts were made from the observation deck in the building's early years, the problem wasn't addressed until a jumper injured a pedestrian upon landing in January 1947. This near miss, coupled with a rash of suicide attempts that year, forced the building's owners to erect a high fence strong enough to deter future jumpers. But that hasn't stopped the spirits of those who succeeded from lingering on the observation deck, usually late at night.

Most of the spirits seen by workers and tourists are of the generic variety—white, filmy, and silent. Who they were and why they stayed behind is unknown, but apparitions do seem to roam the building: In fact, many people have reportedly caught glimpses of a ghostly figure that runs straight through the fence and plunges over the edge.

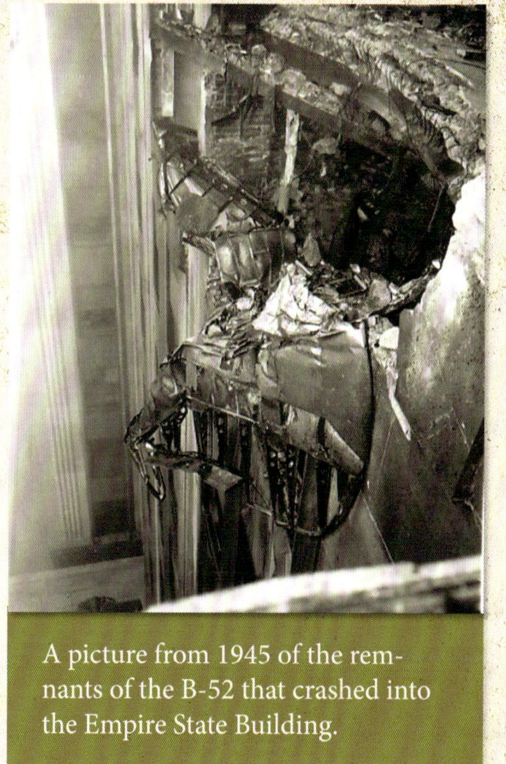

A picture from 1945 of the remnants of the B-52 that crashed into the Empire State Building.

Notice the lack of a barrier surrounding the observation deck. A fence was put in place after several suicide attempts occurred during a three week span in 1947.

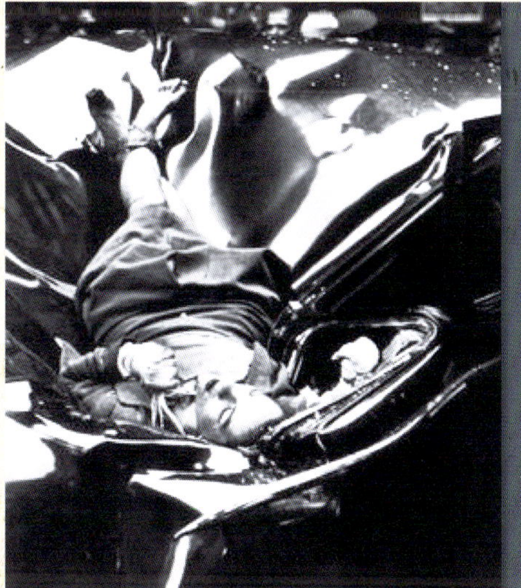

Suicide victim Evelyn McHale jumped from the eighty-sixth-floor observation deck of the Empire State Building in 1947. This observation deck was also the location of a murder-suicide in 1995 where one victim was killed and six wounded.

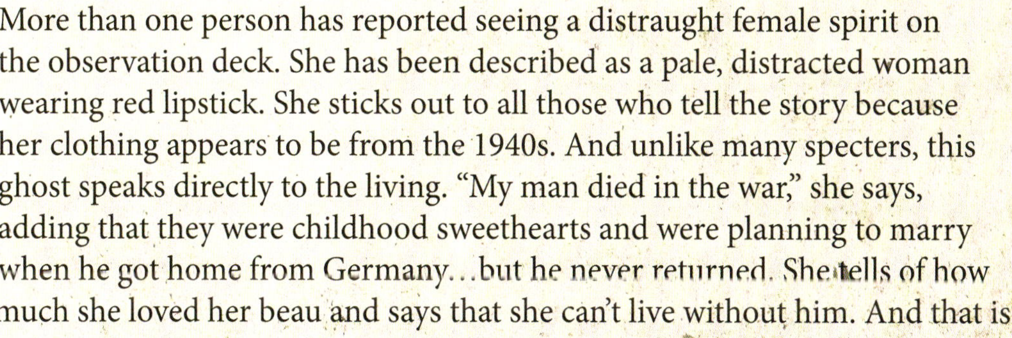

The Ghost of World War II

More than one person has reported seeing a distraught female spirit on the observation deck. She has been described as a pale, distracted woman wearing red lipstick. She sticks out to all those who tell the story because her clothing appears to be from the 1940s. And unlike many specters, this ghost speaks directly to the living. "My man died in the war," she says, adding that they were childhood sweethearts and were planning to marry when he got home from Germany…but he never returned. She tells of how much she loved her beau and says that she can't live without him. And that is apparently what drove the woman over the edge—literally. One visitor, who encountered the ghostly woman in 1985, actually saw her plunge over the wall, only to return a short time later to tell the same story in the exact same words to another unsuspecting tourist.

Every day, visitors go to the Empire State Building to admire the wonderful Art Deco architecture and take in the spectacular view of New York City and the surrounding area. But if you ever visit the building, keep an eye out for the poor souls that remain there. And if you use your camera, be sure to check your pictures carefully: That white blob may not be a photographic error after all.

The Haunted Destroyer
(Buffalo, New York)

Shortly after the Japanese attack on Pearl Harbor, five brothers from Waterloo, Iowa—George, Francis, Joseph, Madison, and Albert Sullivan—enlisted in the U.S. Navy and served together aboard the light cruiser USS *Juneau*. Sadly, their inspiring story of family patriotism turned tragic when the *Juneau* was sunk by a Japanese submarine in November 1942, sending all five Sullivan brothers to a watery grave. Their story was immortalized in the movie *The Fighting Sullivans* (1944) and served as an inspiration for Steven Spielberg's *Saving Private Ryan* (1998).

In 1943, the navy honored the Sullivan brothers by naming a destroyer after them: USS *The Sullivans*. It was a proud ship that served valiantly during the remainder of World War II, in the Korean War, and then in various hot spots around the world as part of the 6th Fleet. But after the vessel was decommissioned in 1965, the navy had a difficult time finding people willing to clean and maintain it. The reason? The spirits of the Sullivan brothers were apparently haunting the ship.

The Sullivans received nine battle stars for its service in World War II and one star for its Korean War service.

Haunted Happenings Begin

The ghosts were quiet while the ship was on active duty, but they started making themselves known upon its retirement. Those who worked aboard *The Sullivans* after it was decommissioned reported seeing flying objects and hearing weird sounds and terrifying moans. Fleeting glimpses of young men dressed in World War II-era naval uniforms were also common sights.

One of the first acknowledgments that something bizarre was occurring aboard *The Sullivans* came when an electrician's mate refused an order to make a routine check of the ship. It was Friday the 13th he explained, and the last time he had been aboard the ship on that traditionally superstitious day, an unseen hand had reached out from a bulkhead, grabbed him by the ankle, and tripped him.

The Sullivan brothers died in the Naval Battle of Guadalcanal when their ship, the USS *Juneau*, was sunk by a Japanese submarine on November 13, 1942. Pictured here from left to right are Joseph, Francis, Albert, Madison, and George.

More Incidents Revealed

After the sailor's story was made public, others came forward with tales of their own frightening encounters aboard the destroyer. Another electrician's mate reported that something had reached out and snatched away the toolbox he had been carrying, and another sailor claimed that five glowing spheres passed him in a darkened hatchway while he stood paralyzed with fear.

In another account, a sailor assigned to work on the vessel said that he felt a chill and a sense of dread the moment he set foot aboard the ship. Within minutes, he was having trouble breathing, and he experienced an odd buzzing in his ears. "I felt like I had stepped into another world, and it wasn't a world where I wanted to be," said the sailor, who, until that day, had never believed in ghosts. "I knew there and then that I was never going back aboard that ship."

Most of the supernatural phenomena reported aboard *The Sullivans* occurred while the destroyer was docked in Philadelphia. For reasons unknown, removing the ship from active service apparently triggered a tremendous amount of activity from the spirits of the five Sullivan brothers. When the ship was relocated, however, ghost sightings and paranormal activity slowed dramatically.

Now a Museum

In 1977, *The Sullivans* was donated to the Buffalo and Erie County Naval & Military Park in Buffalo, New York, where it was turned into a memorial museum that is open for public tours. In 1986, the fabled vessel was declared a National Historic Landmark.

The story of the five Sullivan brothers and their untimely deaths captured the nation's attention and led to immediate policy changes within the U.S. Navy, which worked to ensure that no American family would ever again suffer such a grave loss. The story of the ship's haunting isn't well known outside of the small fraternity of people who worked aboard the vessel and experienced the brothers' spirited antics firsthand. Why the restless spirits of the brothers manifested when they did, did what they did, and then quieted down remains a mystery.

The USS *Juneau's* service was very short. It was built in 1940, launched in October of 1941, commissioned in February of 1942, and sunk in November of 1942. A total of 687 men died when the *Juneau* was sunk at Ironbottom Sound in the Solomon Islands.

The USS *The Sullivans* (DD-537) positioned alongside the USS *Ajax*. The *Ajax* was decommissioned and scrapped in 1986. It had received four battle stars for its service in the Korean War.

New Jersey's

Haunted Union Hotel

(Flemington, New Jersey)

A New Jersey hotel that witnessed a major event continues to make history of its own–haunted history, that is.

The Union Hotel was first constructed in 1814 by Neal Hart. Hart intended the hotel to be a place for affluent stagecoach passengers to congregate in the 19th century. The exterior of the building was renovated in 1878, while the interior has been redeveloped many times for various purposes since the hotel closed.

A Shocking Event

In early 1932, in an event that was as sad as it was sensational, Charles Lindbergh—the first man to fly solo across the Atlantic Ocean—again made headlines; however, this time it was for something that would have anything but a happy ending. On the night of March 1, 1932, the famous flyer's twenty-month-old son was kidnapped from the family home in Hopewell, New Jersey. Although Lindbergh paid the requested ransom, the boy's body was eventually found half-buried in a roadside thicket not far from his home. Suspect Bruno Richard Hauptmann, a carpenter and small-time crook, was taken into custody on September 19, 1934. A transfixed American public anxiously awaited Hauptmann's trial, which was scheduled to begin on January 3, 1935, at the Hunterdon County courthouse in Flemington, New Jersey.

Charles Lindbergh giving his testimony during the capital murder trial, the "Trial of the Century," of Richard Hauptmann.

The Trial of the Century

Due to Lindbergh's fame and the revolting nature of the crime, the five-week proceeding was dubbed the "Trial of the Century." As such, it drew members of the press like moths to a flame. To keep reporters close to the action, the Union Hotel, which was located just across the street from the Hunterdon County courthouse, was tapped as the press headquarters. The Victorian building was an apt choice: Built in 1814, the four-story hotel was near the site of the trial, and it had a bar on its premises—just the thing to soothe battle-weary correspondents looking to unwind. On February 13, 1935, the jury handed down a guilty verdict, which carried with it the death penalty. Happy that the villain had received his due, Americans rejoiced. Hauptmann went to the electric chair on April 3, 1936. Since that day, however, speculation regarding his culpability in the crime has stirred relentlessly. But that's not the only thing that's been stirring.

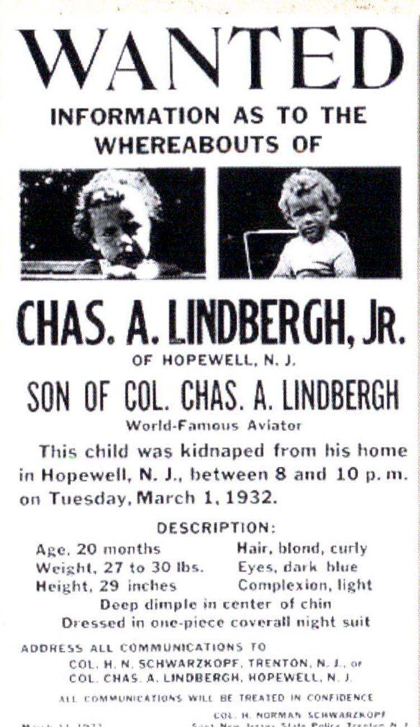
WANTED

INFORMATION AS TO THE WHEREABOUTS OF

CHAS. A. LINDBERGH, JR.

OF HOPEWELL, N. J.

SON OF COL. CHAS. A. LINDBERGH

World-Famous Aviator

This child was kidnaped from his home in Hopewell, N. J., between 8 and 10 p. m. on Tuesday, March 1, 1932.

DESCRIPTION:

Age, 20 months	Hair, blond, curly
Weight, 27 to 30 lbs.	Eyes, dark blue
Height, 29 inches	Complexion, light

Deep dimple in center of chin

Dressed in one-piece coverall night suit

ADDRESS ALL COMMUNICATIONS TO
COL. H. N. SCHWARZKOPF, TRENTON, N. J., or
COL. CHAS. A. LINDBERGH, HOPEWELL, N. J.

ALL COMMUNICATIONS WILL BE TREATED IN CONFIDENCE

COL. H. NORMAN SCHWARZKOPF
Supt. New Jersey State Police, Trenton, N. J.

March 11, 1932

Charles Jr.'s body was found on May 12, 1932, by a delivery truck driver, William Allen, who had pulled to the side of the road to relieve himself. The child's skull had been fractured. There were also signs of a badly executed burial at the scene.

Most of the paranormal activity in the Union Hotel has taken place in the upper levels of the hotel where the public is seldomly allowed to enter.

Harrowing Happenings

After the press departed the Union Hotel, little more was heard about the inn—little more of an earthly nature, that is. Staff reports of paranormal occurrences began trickling in, with each story sounding just a tad more terrifying than the one that preceded it. Over the years, several businesses have opened in the building—most recently a restaurant, which closed in 2008. According to witnesses, the ghosts of the Union Hotel have a penchant for vigorously spinning barstools. After this gets the attention of the intended eyewitness, which it unfailingly does, their next trick is to slam doors…loudly.

One night after closing, a bouncer locked the doors to the hotel's foyer and then joined staff members for a drink. Suddenly, the doors flew open—completely unaided—and a cold breeze blew past the group. Dumbfounded by what he had witnessed, the bouncer again closed the doors. As he did, he saw a phantom pair of children's shoes scrambling up the main stairway. Horrified, he turned and fled.

In another incident, a waitress was carrying her cash drawer upstairs after closing. As she reached the top step, she heard a disembodied voice humming a lullaby. Like the bouncer, she fled the scene, never to return again.

Spirits and Other Spirits

At least one ghost at the Union Hotel has its disembodied heart in the right place. While going over her books late one night, a night manager sensed a sudden presence. Startled, she moved back from her desk, and an invisible intruder moved up against her and pressed against her chest. She asked it to move away and the ghost respectfully complied. While some might categorize this turn of events as fortunate, the woman isn't so sure: She regrets telling the entity to back away for fear that she may never have such an encounter again. Had the manager met the ghost of the condemned man? It's doubtful, since Hauptmann never stayed at the hotel. It's more likely that she brushed up against the spirit of a reporter left over from the days of the Hauptmann trial that was feeling a little frisky after unwinding in the bar.

Meet the Ghosts of Owl's Head Light (Owls Head, Maine)

No one is sure exactly when the hauntings began, but at some point, caretakers began finding human footprints in the snow on the stairway that leads from the caretaker's house to the tower. The footprints started about halfway up the stairs, as if someone had materialized on the spot. Whoever made the prints had a purpose: The tracks often led to an open lighthouse door, and caretakers would find a fresh shine on the equipment inside.

The original Owl's Head Light was commissioned and built in 1825 after a boom in the lime-mining industry in nearby Rockland increased shipping traffic around the bay's rocky shores. A sturdier structure replaced the poorly-built original lighthouse in 1852, but it wasn't until recent times that ghosts began to visit the promontory.

Bedroom Invader

One strange incident happened around 1985, when lighthouse keeper Andy Germann got up late one night to tend to some chores that he'd forgotten to do outside the house. As he left the bedroom, Andy saw a misty form float over the floor and pass into the room. He shrugged it off—figuring that it was just the bay's formidable fog—and continued with his task. Andy's wife Denise was trying to get back to sleep when she felt her husband lie down on his side of the bed. But when she turned to ask why he had returned so quickly, all she could see was a body-sized dent on the mattress. The impression could conceivably have been leftover from when Andy exited the bed…except that it kept changing in depth, as if someone was fidgeting to get comfortable. This continued for several minutes before Denise surmised that it was the work of a ghostly intruder, and she kindly asked it to leave. It did, but other strange phenomena—such as doors opening and closing on their own and the sound of footsteps—continued to occur, especially in a particular upstairs room. Only a few years later, new residents received a clue about who might have been making tracks in the snow, cleaning the great lighthouse lens, and trying to sleep in the main bedroom. After caretaker

Gerard Graham, his wife Debbie, and their young daughter Claire moved into the structure, Claire would often describe a playmate that only she could see. He looked like an old-fashioned sea captain, she said. Claire began to spout technical nautical terms that her parents said she did not know, and she even warned her father when the foghorn needed to be turned on. Incidentally, Claire slept in the bedroom that the Germanns believed was haunted.

The Frozen Couple

In 1850, a great storm lashed the bay a few days before Christmas. A small schooner anchored at a neighboring port was having a hard time in the crashing waves, and its captain left the vessel, perhaps to seek help.

Before the captain returned, the schooner's cables snapped and the storm propelled it toward Rockland Harbor. Aboard the schooner were three hapless souls: the first mate, Richard Ingraham; Ingraham's fiancée, Lydia Dyer; and a sailor, Roger Elliott. It did not take long before the vessel crashed aground near Owl's Head Light. It remained partially intact, but freezing water quickly drenched the three passengers, who were huddled together under blankets that began to collect ice.

Thawed Out

The engaged couple eventually lost consciousness, but Elliott managed to get off the ship and clamber over the rocks to the lighthouse. Fortunately, the caretaker passed by on a horse-drawn sleigh and saw the half-frozen man, who told him of his capsized friends.

Both appeared to be dead, but their seemingly lifeless bodies were chipped out and brought back to the caretaker's home, although it took great effort to release the couple from their icy tomb. The rescuers then managed to thaw the pair out by pouring water on them and rubbing their arms and legs to restore circulation. Much to the surprise and joy of all present, Ingraham and Dyer regained consciousness. They eventually married as planned and raised four children.

Elliott was not so lucky; he died, possibly of hypothermia. No one knows for sure what happened to the schooner's captain. Perhaps he never made it ashore to seek help but ultimately found comfort in the caretaker's house, where he visited young Claire Graham more than a hundred years later.

Over the years, a strange white figure has been seen to appeared in a window of the lighthouse. One caretaker's child reported seeing a mysterious woman sitting on a bedroom chair, and several caretakers claimed that they glimpsed a small spectral woman working in the kitchen. To make her presence known, the ghostly cook likes to jangle tableware and slam cupboard doors.

The keeper's house was built in 1854 and now serves as the headquarters of the American Lighthouse Foundation.

Tormented Spirits at the Lizzie Borden Bed & Breakfast (Fall River, Massachusetts)

"Lizzie Borden took an ax And gave her mother forty whacks,/ And when she saw what she had done,/ She gave her father forty-one."

This poem has been a schoolyard staple for more than a century; however, it contains a few errors. For example, it states that Lizzie Borden whacked her mother with an ax forty times before turning on her father. In reality, the Bordens were murdered with a hatchet, not an ax. And Mrs. Borden suffered around twenty wounds while her husband suffered eleven—still more than enough to kill them both. What's more, Abby Borden was Lizzie's stepmother, not her mother.

But the poem may have yet another inaccuracy: Lizzie Borden may not have been the murderer at all!

Today the Lizzie Borden house has become a bed and breakfast where guests can fully immerse themselves in its gruesome past.

Father's Dead!

Lizzie Borden grew up in Fall River, Massachusetts. In 1892, when the murders took place, Lizzie was still living at home at age thirty-two, which was old enough to be considered a spinster by the standards of the day.

On August 4, 1892, the family's maid, Bridget Sullivan, was in her upstairs room when she heard Lizzie screaming. "Come down quick!" Lizzie shouted. "Father's dead! Someone's come in and killed him!"

Andrew Borden was lying dead on the couch, the victim of multiple hatchet wounds. By some accounts, he had been rolled over to look like he was merely sleeping, but there was blood everywhere.

While neighbors tended to the shocked Lizzie, she was asked where she had been when all of this happened. She replied that she had gone to the barn to get something.

A little while later, the police found the body of Abby Borden in a guest room. She was even more mutilated than her husband.

Lizzie was the only person who the police ever arrested for the crime. A great deal of tension had existed between Lizzie and her father, for a variety of reasons. For example, Andrew's decision to divide his property among his relatives, rather than among his children, had caused much strife within the family. Also, he had recently killed Lizzie's pet pigeons, which he said had become a nuisance; he decapitated them and left the bodies for Lizzie to find.

Not long before the murders, Andrew had suspected that he was being poisoned. However, he didn't know who to accuse; after all, his miserly ways and shrewd business dealings had made him very unpopular in town—the culprit could have been almost anyone. But few people get poisoned simply for being unpopular, and Lizzie had been spotted buying cyanide at a local pharmacy just days before the murders. This made her look fairly suspicious.

In addition, Lizzie's explanation—that she had been in the barn while the murders took place—didn't convince everyone. For one thing, the bodies looked like they'd been moved. And how long could it possibly have taken her to get something out of the barn?

The Lizzie Borden house is the most famous structure in the Corky Row Historic District. Visitors can go and see it at 230 Second Street, Fall River, Massachusetts.

FRANK LESLIE'S
ILLUSTRATED
WEEKLY

The trial lasted fifteen days in June of 1893 in New Bedford, MA, ending with Lizzie's acquittal. The trial and the media frenzy around it is comparable only to the seminal trials of O.J. Simpson, Ethel and Julius Rosenberg, and Richard Hauptmann.

The Verdict

Lizzie was arrested for the murders, although the evidence against her was slim. There were no bloodstains on her dress when the police arrived on the scene, and no bloody clothes were ever found. A broken hatchet was located in the basement, but it could not be connected to the murders. With no solid evidence, the jury deliberated just ninety minutes before acquitting her.

After the trial, Lizzie changed her name to "Lizbeth" and went on with her life. She lived a somewhat lavish lifestyle in her new home, which she called Maplecroft, until her death in 1927.

Today, there are dozens of theories about the identity of the actual killer. Some say that it was Lizzie, while others think that it wasn't her but that she knew very well who it was. Still others believe that Lizzie had nothing to do with it. The sad truth is that we'll probably never know for sure who committed the crime. But the ghosts of Andrew and Abby Borden may want to keep the investigation alive.

Can You Still Hear the Screams?

Years after the crime, the Borden House became a museum/bed-and-breakfast that was made to look almost exactly as it did at the time of the murders. Guests can actually sleep in the very room in which Abby Borden was killed and eat a breakfast of bananas, coffee, and johnnycakes, just like Mr. and Mrs. Borden did on that fateful morning before their brutal deaths.

Ghost sightings in the old green Victorian house are common—MSNBC even listed the house among the top ten most haunted houses in the United States.

The most active ghost there seems to be that of Abby Borden. Many guests have reported hearing the sound of a woman weeping in the bedroom where Abby's body was found. Many others have heard the sound of footsteps, and some have even reported that as they lay in their beds, an older woman in an old-fashioned Victorian-era dress has come into the room to tuck them in for the night.

But Abby is not the only ghost that roams the B & B. Guests have also occasionally spotted Andrew, and he has also manifested during séances that have been held at the house.

Lizzie's spirit has also been seen at the Borden home. From time to time, guests see a ghostly woman carrying a sharp weapon. Could this be Lizzie—or is it the real murderer?

The murder of Andrew and Abby Borden has yet to be solved. People still speculate the identity of the killer, citing Lizzie herself, Bridget Sullivan, William Borden (Andrew's illegitimate son), Lizzie's sister Emma Borden, or Lizzie's uncle John Morse as the culprits. This is a scene of both Lizzie and Emma at the trial.

Although the Bordens were a relatively affluent family for the time, Andrew Borden was a frugal man. The house lacked indoor plumbing on the first and second floors and was closer to the inner-city than the more wealthy and homegenous area, The Hill, where many cousins of the Borden family lived. After the trials Emma and Lizzie both moved to The Hill neighborhood in a house Lizzie called Maplecroft.

Whoever they are, the ghosts at the Lizzie Borden Bed & Breakfast certainly aren't shy. Many guests have captured strange photos, videos, and audio recordings that feature unusual blobs of light, sounds resembling screams, and shadows that simply shouldn't be there. The owner of the house admits to being touched and pushed by unseen hands. And in 2008, a couple visiting on the anniversary of the brutal murders fled the B & B in terror after the door to their room flung open by itself and a lamp moved and lit up on its own. There are many haunted hotels around the world, but few generate as much paranormal activity as the Lizzie Borden Bed & Breakfast.

But allegedly, the Bordens don't just haunt their former home. People have seen mysterious lights at Oak Grove Cemetery, where the family is buried. And a few folks have even heard screams coming from the Borden plot, where Lizzie's body lies right next to the remains of her father and stepmother.

Andrew's body was found on the couch in the downstairs sitting room. The investigation believes Andrew was asleep when he was attacked because one of his eyeballs had been split in half. The murder took place a short time before his body was found because his wounds were still bleeding.

According to the investigation, it is said that Abby Borden was facing her killer when she was first struck with the hatchet on the side of her head. The first blow caused contusions on her nose and forehead, leading Abby to fall face down. The killer then struck Abby multiple times in the back of the head.

Lizzie Borden was ostricized from the Fall River community after the trial. She changed her name to Lizabeth and lived in relative obscurity until her name became popular in the news again when she was caught shoplifting in Rhode Island.

Fort Warren's Lady in Black
(Georges Island, Massachusetts)

In the opening days of the Civil War—the days of unrealistic expectations, when many thought that the war would be over in a matter of weeks or months—Andrew Lanier was preparing to leave his home in Georgia to serve in the Confederate Army. But before he left, he asked his beloved girlfriend Melanie to marry him. She did, and the two spent just one night together as husband and wife. The next day, Andrew headed off to war, undoubtedly assuming that he would return home soon. Little did either of them know that they would never again see each other as a free man and woman.

A few months later, Andrew was captured by Union forces and was sent to Fort Warren, a military prison on Georges Island, which is located about seven miles off the coast of Boston. As military prisons go, Fort Warren was not as bad as some others, but to Lanier it was intolerable. He deeply missed Georgia and his wife, and he shared these sentiments with her in a letter.

After Melanie read the letter, she knew that she could not stand by idly while her husband rotted away in prison. So she cut her hair short, disguised herself as a man, and made her way across Union lines to Massachusetts. Finally, during a violent storm, she managed to slip inside the prison, which was not terribly secure. (It was thought that even if a prisoner escaped from Fort Warren, he would have nowhere to go since he was on an island seven miles from land.) Soon, Melanie was reunited with her husband.

It took nearly three decades to build Fort Warren. It opened in the early days of the Civil War in 1861 and defended Boston Harbor until the end of World War II.

Foiled and Spoiled

The fort's other prisoners were likely pleased to see a Southern woman in their midst. They were certainly happy that she had brought along an old pistol and a short-handled pick. The prisoners hatched a scheme to tunnel underneath the fort's arsenal; once there, they planned to grab guns and seize the fort. Then they would turn the fort's artillery on Boston.

The prisoners worked on the tunnel for the next few weeks. However, they had miscalculated the distance to the arsenal, so when they tried to break through the ground, they were caught. One by one, they came out of the tunnel—except for Melanie. She had planned to wait until all of the others had been accounted for and then pop out of the hole with her pistol and take the guards by surprise.

It was a long shot, but it might have worked. Unfortunately for the Confederate prisoners, after Melanie emerged from the hole and ordered the guards to surrender, they quickly formed a circle around her and closed in. Just as Melanie pulled the trigger on her gun, it was knocked from her hand; the wayward bullet struck her husband and killed him instantly. Melanie was captured and was sentenced to hang as a Rebel spy.

On the day of her execution, Melanie made a final request: She wanted to wear a woman's dress for the hanging instead of the men's clothing that she had been wearing for weeks. She was given an old black dress that had been used for a theatrical performance at the fort. That should have been the end...but it was only the beginning.

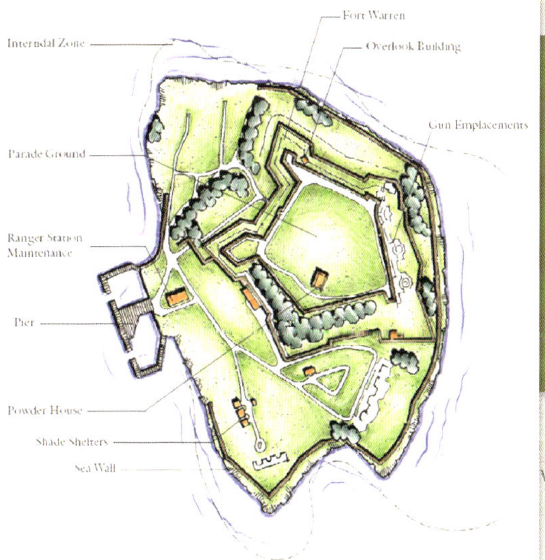

Fort Warren was a part of the third system of U.S. fortifications, which was a seacoast defense system that used submarine minefields, nets and booms, and forts to defend America's coastline. Since airplanes were not yet a threat to national security, seacoast defense was a major concern for America after it gained its independence.

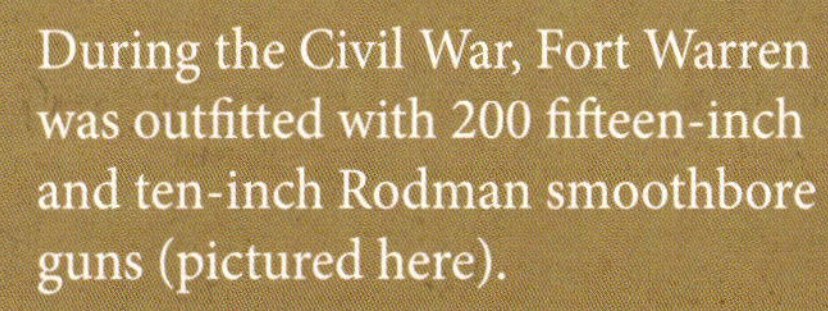

During the Civil War, Fort Warren was outfitted with 200 fifteen-inch and ten-inch Rodman smoothbore guns (pictured here).

Un-"fort"-unate Occurrences

A short time later, a soldier named Cassidy was patrolling the area near where Melanie had been executed. Suddenly, he felt two hands grab him around the neck from behind. The hands began to squeeze, trying to strangle him. Struggling for breath, Cassidy managed to twist around so that he could see his attacker: He was staring into the ghostly face of Melanie Lanier.

Clad in the black dress in which she had died, Melanie was staring sinisterly at the soldier, her face pale but her eyes ablaze with hatred and revenge. Cassidy screamed, and managed to twist out of her grip. He then ran back to the other guards, crying out in terror. But not only did his story provoke fits of laughter, it also got him locked away in the guardhouse for thirty days for deserting his post. That was fine with Cassidy, who vowed never to patrol that area after dark again.

The "Lady in Black" has been haunting Fort Warren ever since then. In 1891, female footprints were found in the snow, even though no woman had been on the island. Then, during World War II, an army sentry encountered the ghost of Melanie Lanier near the site where she had died. He was so frightened by the incident that he went insane and spent the next two decades in a mental institution.

Fort Warren imprisoned many high-ranking Confederate officers like John Gregg, Adam "Stovepipe" Johnson, and Lloyd Tigham. Many Confederate civilians were held there as well, including Confederate Vice-President Alexander Stephens and Confederate Postmaster General John Henninger Reagan.

A photo of Fort Warren in 1861.

A few years after World War II, Captain Charles Norris was stationed alone on the island. He was reading one night when he felt someone tap him on the shoulder. He turned around, but no one was there.

Later, when the telephone began to ring, Norris answered it only to hear the male operator ask, "What number please?"

Norris explained that he was answering a call, not making one. The operator said that Norris's wife had answered the phone previously and had taken a message. All alone on the island, Norris knew that only one female could have answered the phone: The Lady in Black.

The vengeful wraith still roams Fort Warren. Sentries on duty there have been known to shoot at ill-defined forms, and once, a stone rolled all the way across a floor under its own power. It seems that Melanie Lanier is still trying to devise ways to distract the guards stationed there. After all, it was her love for her husband that brought her to the island, and even though they're both long dead, her love—like her spirit—lives on.

The fort was owned by the federal government until 1958 when the state of Massachusetts bought it. It was opened to the public in 1961 after minor restoration.

Fort Warren was known as a humane Confederate prison in contrast to similar institutions of the time. When Fort Warren's camp commander's son, Lieutenant Justin E. Dimick, left the fort for active duty, he was given a note by the Confederate officers in the camp that ordered for his good care if he were to be captured and imprisoned by the Confederates.

The Hoosac Tunnel
(Williamstown, Massachusetts)

By the mid-1800s, the train was the preeminent form of transportation in America, and competition between railroad lines was fierce. If a means could be found to shorten a route, create a link, or speed up a journey, it was generally taken to help ensure a railroad's continued profitability. In 1848, the newly formed Troy and Greenfield Railroad proposed a direct route that would link Greenfield and Williamstown, Massachusetts. In Williamstown, it would connect to an existing route on which trains could travel to Troy, New York, and points west. The time-saving measure seemed like a brilliant move, except for one not-so-small detail: Between Greenfield and Williamstown stood a forbidding promontory known as Hoosac Mountain. In order to tame it, the railroad would need to drill a tunnel—but not just any tunnel: At nearly five miles in length, it would have to be the world's longest tunnel.

The Great Bore

In 1851, the project was set in motion. Almost immediately, trouble arose when drillers learned that the soft rock stratum through which they were supposed to be boring was, in fact, harder than nails. In 1861, funding dried up, and by 1862—realizing that it had bitten off more than it could chew—the Troy and Greenfield Railroad defaulted on its loan. The state of Massachusetts stepped in to complete the tunnel.

With a steady infusion of cash and a government bent on completing the project, the Hoosac Tunnel was finally finished in 1873; in 1876, the "Great Bore" officially opened for business. The project had taken a quarter century to complete at a total cost of $21 million. Nearly 200 lives were lost while the tunnel was built, with thirteen being the result of an incident that's legendary to this day.

Aside from all of the other engineering challenges the engineers faced in the tunnel's construction, the greatest challenge was to align the four compartments of the tunnel when they met. Engineers dug in from the western and eastern ends and also in both directions from the central shaft. When the central shaft met with the eastern portal, they were aligned within 9/16 inch.

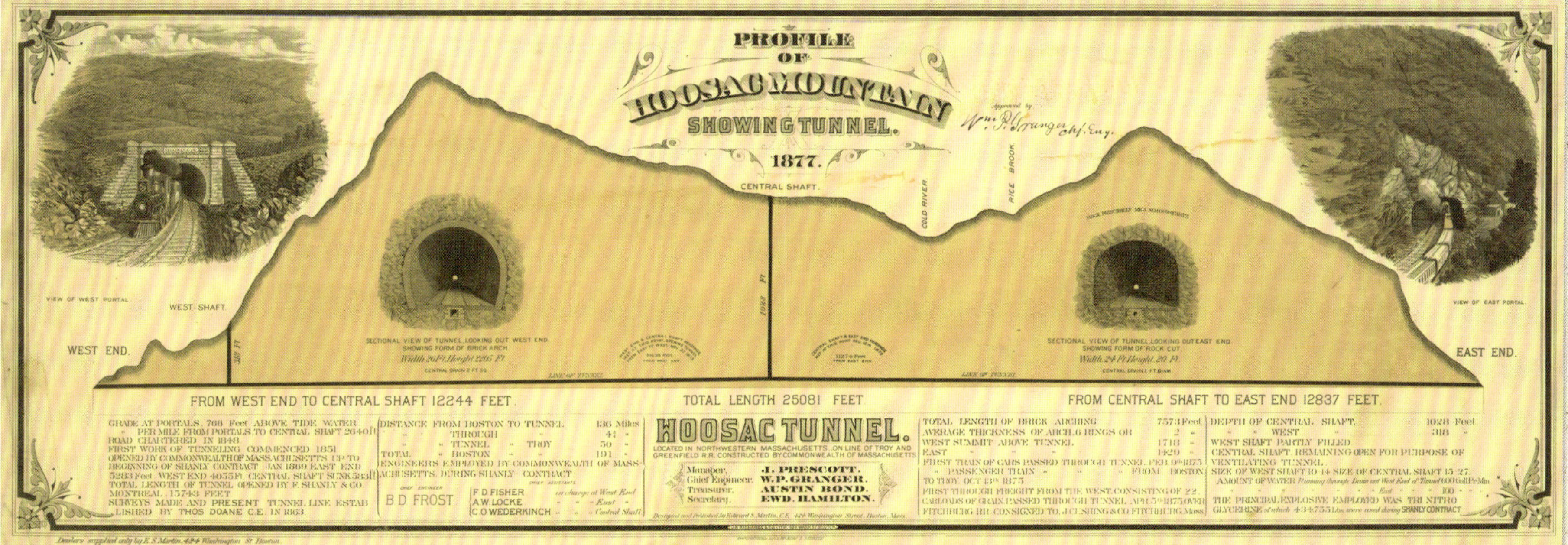

Tragedy Strikes

The excavation of the tunnel required the removal of two million long tons of rock.

It happened on October 17, 1867, inside the tunnel's central shaft—a vertical hole that was drilled from atop the mountain to intersect with the midpoint of the tunnel 1,028 feet below. The shaft would supply much-needed ventilation to the tunnel and allow drillers two more facings from which to attack, a measure that would greatly speed up operations.

On this particular day, the shaft reached into the mountain some 538 feet. While attempting to light a lamp, a workman accidentally ignited a gasoline tank. Within seconds, an inferno rocketed up to the surface, claiming the pumping station and hoist house located above, causing them to collapse into the deep pit. Unfortunately, thirteen men were working in the shaft during the incident. As soon as was humanly possible, a miner was lowered into the smoldering cavity to search for survivors; he passed out during the long trip but managed to gasp "no hope" upon his return to the surface.

Without an operational pump, the cavity eventually filled to the brim with seepage and rainwater. It wasn't until a year later that the central shaft gave up its grisly contents. As it turns out, most of the victims hadn't died from the flames or from drowning: The stranded men had built a survival raft but were slowly asphyxiated by the poisonous gases and the oxygen-hungry flames raging above them.

Spirits Rise

In a 1985 article, Glenn Drohan—a reporter for the *North Adams Transcript*—told of strange phenomena at the tunnel, such as "vague shapes and muffled wails near the water-filled pit." Shortly after the accident occurred, workmen allegedly saw the spirits of the lost miners carrying picks and shovels. The workers called out to the missing men, but they did not answer, and their apparitions quickly vanished.

Other tragic goings-on at the Hoosac Tunnel include the strange death of Ringo Kelley. In 1865, when explosive nitroglycerin was first used for excavation, experts Kelley, Billy Nash, and Ned Brinkman attempted to set a charge of nitro before running for cover. Nash and Brinkman never made it: Kelley somehow set off the explosion prematurely, burying his coworkers in the process.

A view of the tunnel's east portal. The constuction process saw the death of 193 workers before the tunnel opened, leading many survivors to dub the tunnel the "Blood Pit." Many died in explosions from black powder and nitroglycerin (which was being commercially used for the first time in the U.S. for the Hoosac project).

Shortly thereafter, Kelley vanished. He was not seen again until March 30, 1866, when his lifeless body was found two miles inside the tunnel. Bizarrely, he had been strangled to death at the precise spot where Nash and Brinkman had perished. Investigators never developed any leads, but workmen had an ominous feeling about Kelley's demise: They believed that the vengeful spirits of Nash and Brinkman had done him in.

Present-Day Poltergeists

If the preceding tales seem quaint due to the passage of time, it's worth noting that the tunnel still features its share of hauntings; standouts among these are railroad worker Joseph Impoco's trio of supernatural tales. In an article that appeared in *The Berkshire Sampler* on October 30, 1977, Impoco told reporter Eileen Kuperschmid that he was chipping ice from the tracks one day when he heard a voice say, "Run, Joe, run!" As Impoco tells it, "I turned, and sure enough, there was No. 60 coming at me. Boy, did I jump back fast! When I looked [back], there was no one there."

Six weeks later, Impoco was working with an iron crowbar, doing his best to free cars that were stuck to the icy tracks. Suddenly, he heard, "Joe! Joe! Drop it, Joe!" He instinctively dropped the crowbar just as 11,000 volts of electricity struck it from a short-circuited power line overhead.

In the final incident, Impoco was removing trees from the tunnel's entrance when, from out of nowhere, an enormous oak fell directly toward him. He managed to outrun the falling tree, but he heard a frightening, ethereal laugh as he ran; he was certain that it hadn't come from any of his coworkers.

Currently, nearly twelve trains a day pass through the Hoosac Tunnel. Not too many considering the 70,000 cars that were passing through the tunnel every month in 1913.

Travel Tips

For the brave at heart, a visit to the Hoosac Tunnel can prove awe-inspiring and educational. The tunnel is still used, so walking inside it is strictly off-limits, but a well-worn path beside the tracks leads to the Hoosac's entrance. For those who are looking to avoid things that go bump in the night, a trip to the nearby North Adams' Hoosac Tunnel Museum in the Western Gateway Heritage State Park will reveal the incredible history of this five-mile-long portal into another dimension—and will do so far away from Ringo Kelley's haunts. All aboard!

Ghosts in the Witch City
(Salem, Massachusetts)

One of the darkest chapters in American history, the Salem Witch Trials have haunted our country for more than 300 years. Numerous plays and movies have recounted the tale of two young girls from Massachusetts who, in 1692, wrongfully accused people in their town of witchcraft. This sparked a mass hysteria that led to charges against hundreds and the executions of twenty innocent people. The lessons learned from this miscarriage of justice have stuck with the people of the United States, but so have the restless spirits of the victims of this tragedy.

Nineteen people were sent to the gallows as a result of the Salem Witch Trials. All of those who were accused and charged never admitted to practicing witchcraft and maintained their innocence up until they were put to death. Five others died in prison (including two infants).

The Last House

Today, the people of Salem, Massachusetts, acknowledge the crimes of the past, and the town recognizes its history in many ways, from witch logos on its police cars to a number of kitschy attractions erected solely to attract tourists. Among the gift shops and New Age bookstores, only one building with a connection to the trials remains: Known locally as "The Witch House," Judge Jonathan Corwin's former home still hosts visitors on Essex Street. Some of those visiting the historic site are overcome with feelings of anxiety, fear, and anger—all emotions likely experienced by those Corwin sentenced to death. Some have seen the apparition of a woman lingering in the bedrooms on the second floor, and others have witnessed a couple that vanishes into thin air while walking the grounds. Some employees report strange noises after hours, including what sounds like the shuffling of feet on the floorboards and the dragging of furniture from one room to another. The spirits of The Witch House have even been captured on film, although most appear to be little more than manifestations of light or swirling mists.

No executions or trials were held in Judge Corwin's Witch House.

The Gallows

Judge Corwin's former home is not the only place in Salem where the spirits of those he condemned make their presence known. Photographs of orbs and mists that are similar to those snapped at The Witch House have been taken in the area once known as Gallows Hill. Though precise records of where the accused were hanged no longer exist, many believe that a playground and basketball court now reside where the town's gallows once stood. This would explain the eerie photographs of apparitions, as well as other strange phenomena that occur at the site. Electronics frequently malfunction there, and it isn't uncommon for people to hear otherworldly crying at the location at night. Some visitors have reported feeling an invisible presence brush up against them, while others have had their hair pulled by an unseen force.

The parsonage where the first reports of witchcraft in Salem came from. It was in this house that Abigail Williams and Betty Paris first went through the fits which were thought to be the result of witchcraft. Elizabeth Hubbard, Sarah Good, and Titube were all accused of afflicting the girls with witchcraft.

Harbinger at Howard Street

Of course, a town as old as Salem inevitably has several cemeteries, and one of the most haunted is Howard Street Cemetery, which sits across from where the old jail once stood. Photographers at the graveyard have captured images of the same unexplainable mists, orbs, and lights that are found at other locations, and reports of physical contact with an invisible entity abound as well. For more than a hundred years now, passersby have witnessed apparitions wandering among the old tombstones. Although most of the graves at the Howard Street Cemetery don't date back further than the 1800s, the site itself is inextricably tied to the witch trials: The graveyard was built on the location where Sheriff George Corwin tried to crush a confession out of Giles Corey—and when Corey's ghost is seen, the entire town of Salem trembles.

Corey was put to death in the field, which would later become Howard Street Cemetery in 1801, across from the jailhouse that held him. He was buried in an unmarkerd grave.

More Weight...

When Anne Putnam accused Giles Corey of appearing to her as a spirit and trying to entice her with his satanic ways, Corey—who was over eighty years old at the time—didn't give the charge much credence. He even briefly supported accusations against his wife until he realized how seriously the charges were being taken. Sheriff Corwin, the son of Judge Jonathan Corwin, was getting rather wealthy off the prosecution of so-called witches in Salem because anyone found guilty of witchcraft was subject to having his or her property seized and redistributed. That placed Giles Corey in a tough situation: If he pleaded guilty to the accusations against him, he would lose everything; at the same time, no one who had pleaded not guilty had been found to be innocent. Either outcome would mean that Corey's sons would not inherit his estate; instead, it would fall into the hands of the sheriff and the other town leaders. Corey did the only thing he could do: He refused to play their game.

Giles Corey was put to death by a method of torture known as *peine forte et dure*, which subjects its victims to increasing amounts of weight, after he failed to confess at his arraignment.

Corey's Curse

Sheriff Corwin attempted to press a plea out of the old man—literally—by placing more and more weight on his chest every time he refused to confess, instead demanding, "More weight!" The act preserved his sons' inheritance but cost Giles Corey his life. Before he died, however, Corey spat at Corwin and sneered, "Damn you, Sheriff! I curse you and Salem!" Since then, sightings of Corey's ghost have meant disaster for the town. The last time he was spotted was in 1914, just before a fire that nearly wiped Salem off the map. The curse doesn't only target the town itself, though: The very position that George Corwin once held is said to be cursed as well. Every sheriff of Salem since Corwin has either died in office or retired due to heart problems. Between the curse of Giles Corey and all the other restless spirits, one wonders why Salem hasn't changed its nickname from "The Witch City" to "The Haunted City."

A Modeſt Enquiry
Into the Nature of
Witchcraft,
AND
How Perſons Guilty of that Crime may be *Convicted*: And the means uſed for their Diſcovery Diſcuſſed, both *Negatively* and *Affirmatively*, according to *SCRIPTURE* and *EXPERIENCE*.

By John Hale,
Paſtor of the Church of Chriſt in *Beverley*,
Anno Domini 1697.

When they ſay unto you, ſeek unto them that have Familiar Spirits and unto Wizzards, that peep, &c. *To the Law and to the Teſtimony; if they ſpeak not according to this word, it is becauſe there is no light in them,* Iſaiah VIII. 19, 20.
That which I ſee not teach thou me, Job 34 32.

OSTON *in* N. E.
B. Green, and *J. Allen*, for
iot under the Town Houſe. 1702

"A Modest Enquiry Into the Nature of Witchcraft, and How Person's Guilty of that Crime may be Convicted: And the means used for their Discovery Discussed both *Negatively* and *Affirmatively* according to Scripture and Experience" by John Hale, an early supporter of the trials who would later denounce them when his wife was accused of witchcraft by seventeen-year-old Mary Herrick.